"Eugene Linden asks the hard, deeply disturbing questions about the priorities of science in a moral society . . . compassionate but hard-nosed and unsentimental."

The Oregonian

"Chronicles the human side of these experiments, spinning a tale of jealous researchers competing for power as financial interests and the relationships between people and chimps intrude on scientific judgments. It gets to be a dramatic story, complete with a villain or two and even a mysterious death."

Psychology Today

"Has applications far beyond the field of animal rights."

In These Times,
Chicago, Ill.

"It has a strong and convincing point of view. . . . The book supplies important evidence that the apes did indeed speak. . . . Linden makes it much easier to believe that the question is not whether the apes were talking, but rather how well they were."

The Philadelphia Inquirer

SILENT PARTNERS

The Legacy of the Ape Language Experiments

Eugene Linden

BALLANTINE BOOKS • NEW YORK

Grateful acknowledgment is made to Academic Press for permission to reprint an excerpt from "Language in the Great Apes: A Critical Review" by Carolyn A. Ristau and Donald Robbins in *Advances in the Study of Behavior* (Vol. 12) pp. 141–255, by J. S. Rosenblatt, R. A. Hinde, C. Beer, and M. C. Busnell (ed.), New York, Academic Press, 1982. Reprinted by permission of Academic Press and the authors.

Library of Congress Catalog Card Number: 85-40739

ISBN 0-345-34234-8

This edition published by arrangement with Times Books, a division of Random House, Inc.

Manufactured in the United States of America

First Ballantine Books Edition: August 1987

Cover photograph: © Suzanne Haldane

This book is dedicated to the apes, our poor relations.

True human goodness, in all its purity and freedom, can come to the fore only when its recipient has no power. Mankind's true moral test, its fundamental test (which lies deeply buried from view), consists of its attitude towards those who are at its mercy: animals. And in this respect mankind has suffered a fundamental debacle, a debacle so fundamental that all others stem from it.

—MILAN KUNDERA,
from *The Unbearable Lightness of Being*

PREFACE

WHEN I WROTE *Apes, Men, and Language* twelve years ago, I quoted a statement of Carl Jung's to describe the opportunity presented by experiments teaching language to apes. Jung once wrote that man remains an enigma to himself because he lacks the means of comparison necessary for self-knowledge. "He knows how to distinguish himself from other animals in point of anatomy and physiology, but as a conscious, reflecting being, gifted with speech, he lacks all criteria for self-judgment. He is on this planet a unique phenomenon which he cannot compare with anything else. The possibility of comparison and hence of self-knowledge would arise only if he could establish relations with quasi-human mammals inhabiting other stars."

Back then I was very much taken with the irony that while Jung looked to the stars, there were creatures right here on earth—apes like Washoe and Lucy and Ally—who offered the means of comparison and path to self-knowledge that Jung wished for. I assumed that accounts of what these and other apes did would eventually percolate through the behavioral science community. As the details of the ways in which apes used sign language became known, I expected that a variety of minds in a host of different disciplines would begin to integrate this information, and that this in turn would produce a great harvest of new ideas about the nature and origins of both language and intelligence. To a degree, I too, was swept up in the spirit of the times.

But today, twelve years after I quoted Jung, we are still looking to the stars for self-knowledge, and we are still ignoring "quasi-human mammals" that might tell us who we are.

And back here on earth some of the apes involved in these experiments have paid a price as we have turned away from them.

—EUGENE LINDEN
September 1985

ACKNOWLEDGMENTS

THIS BOOK was difficult to write. It involved a painful reexamination of events I have written about in previous publications. Moreover, the events described have produced acrimonious disagreements, and many of the human participants were understandably reluctant to cooperate. For that reason I particularly acknowledge the contributions of two people with whom I have had many conversations during the past few years.

Although Dr. Chris O'Sullivan had no desire to reopen old wounds, she cooperated generously on this project, and I believe that she did so because she cares about the welfare of chimpanzees. She was a witness to but not a principal participant in many of the events discussed in this book, and her cooperation turned out to be immensely helpful.

I also would like to thank Dr. James Mahoney. While he is involved in a medical laboratory, he is not an apologist for what he thinks is wrong about our treatment of chimpanzees in medical labs. I respect his courage to look beyond his immediate self-interest and speak candidly and forcefully.

I would also like to thank Brendan Gill for giving me the benefit of his vast fund of wisdom on writing matters, and I am grateful for the keen eye of Cary Ryan, a copy editor who spies and targets inconsistency the way a hawk does a field mouse.

A couple of institutions helped as well in this project. The Virginia Center for the Creative Arts provided a place where I could write the final chapters of this book, and once there, a portable Compaq Plus computer in concert with Microsoft's program called Word provided the technological assistance I needed to efficiently use the time I had in Virginia.

CONTENTS

PART ONE

Signs of
Discontent

CHAPTER ONE

An Unwelcome Mirror

ON JUNE 3, 1982, as a scorching sun rose in the sky, a large, lavishly equipped, modified tractor-trailer truck pulled up the driveway leading into the Institute for Primate Studies in Norman, Oklahoma. Waiting for the truck was a small group of human beings and chimpanzees. A couple of the human group lit their first cigarettes of the day and peered with tired eyes at the truck as it approached. Among the chimpanzees were two— Ally and Nim—who in years past had achieved a certain fame for their role in experiments seeking to determine whether chimpanzees were capable of learning and using American Sign Language, the language of the deaf in North America. Now, still groggy from the sedative that had been used to get them into their traveling cages, Ally, Nim, and a few other chimpanzees looked at the truck. Earlier most of the chimps had come to the bars voluntarily for their injections of ketamine, but one or two had had to be induced into the "squeeze box" to receive the tranquilizer. The crew of the truck consisted

3

of a driver and a handler, both employed by the Buckshire Corporation, the company that moves the greatest number of chimps between various institutions during the course of a year. When the handler was satisfied that the chimps he was receiving were in good condition, the group began loading them aboard the big climate-controlled rig to begin their twenty-eight-hour journey to their new home, the Laboratory for Experimental Medicine and Surgery in Primates—LEMSIP, for short—located near Sterling Forest, New York.

Chimps are on the move in the United States, and as in the case of earlier movements of great apes during the last decade, their travels signal changes in the alien society in which these animals find themselves. Just as an intelligence agent might study railway movement in East Germany in order to deduce strategic and economic policy, so might another type of agent look at ape movements as an indicator of changes in the beliefs and values of the chimps' captors. The great apes are rare—all of them are endangered—and with a few exceptions the 1,700 or so chimps, gorillas, and orangutans in the United States are not moved about for arbitrary reasons.

Chimps are our closest surviving relatives, and what we do with them, and to them, inevitably comments on that relationship, and hence upon our relationship with the animal world in general.

Perhaps because of the closeness of our relationship, we seem to be hypersensitive about these animals and what we do with them. The fact is that they embarrass us: mentioning a chimp may bring on an attack of the giggles or, in more sophisticated company, an awkward smile. Their nature and their fate always seem to be discussed in a charged atmosphere, which makes them, at least indirectly, valuable as a barometer of the temper of the times.

Moreover, if they elicit smiles from the public, they can have a catastrophic effect on those who work with them. They have been known to break up marriages, destroy friendships, and corrupt scientific judgment by inspiring excessive loyalty or excessive dislike. Indeed, they have caused otherwise normal middle-class people to throw over their lives and run away to the jungle. All of which is to say that they have a catalytic effect on the hidden vulnerabilities of the human mind. Like the classic psychoanalysts, they are there—whether in the zoo or in the lab—to be reacted to, and through some mysterious chemistry, once in contact with them, we reveal ourselves.

There are those who wish that apes and the problems they cause would simply go away. And that is one of the reasons that apes are on the move again.

This book is about the diaspora that has followed the decline of ape language studies in the last decade. In particular, it has to do with the fortunes of apes associated with sign-language experiments in Oklahoma. Some of these apes have celebrated names—Washoe, Lucy, Ally, Nim—while others involved in sign-language experiments passed in and out of the spotlight quickly.

These chimps have suffered different fates. Lucy, for example, went from Oklahoma to the jungles of Africa, instead of to the medical lab. Washoe went from Oklahoma to Washington, where she is still the subject of language and other studies. Wherever they have gone, all of the chimps still live, to use Jane Goodall's phrase, "in the shadow of man." When I wrote a book called *Apes, Men, and Language*, I spent some time exploring the implications of the sign-language experiments with regard to the relationship between human beings and animals. What has become of these chimps after the conclusion of their roles as experimental subjects has prompted a revival of my earlier speculations. Their various journeys are a pilgrim's progress through an ambiguous moral and scientific terrain, in which chimpanzees encounter and contend with the embodiments of the various aspects of man's relationship with our animal nature. Indeed, because of a glut of adult male chimps in the United States, some of these involuntary pilgrims will pay with their lives for our uncertainty about who *we* are. Already some "surplus" chimps are being used in "terminal" studies of the disease AIDS in a few medical laboratories.

Apart from any moral questions, the sagas of some of these animals provide stories of devoted, intelligent, and marvelously strong individuals who have had to deal with challenges for which evolution has not fully prepared them.

I have followed the lives of many of these animals for fourteen years. I have watched Lucy, Washoe, Ally, and Nim at various stages of their development, and I have watched Koko, a lowland gorilla, mature. I have also observed the changes that these apes have wrought on the scientists and other people whose lives they have touched. I have both watched and participated in the debate that has continued for fifteen years now about what these experiments mean.

Recently a rather commonplace thing occurred that has given me a point of comparison against which to judge some of the debates of the era of ape language experiments. That event was the birth to my wife, Madelaine, and me of a daughter, Gillian. In contradistinction to a number of observers who weighed the ability of apes to acquire language against the data on children, I found myself watching Gillian and continually being reminded of the first tentative language probings of chimpanzees. The way in which Gillian at eighteen months mixed up pantomimes and words brought to mind the struggle of apes to express ideas when their enthusiasm exceeded their vocabularies.

A combination of events—the renewed movement of chimps from one place to another; the dramatic changes in both the human and animal players in this drama—have brought our curiously mingled destinies back to mind. My interest is not purely academic. I feel a sense of foreboding whenever I hear that a chimp I used to know has been sold for medical experimentation. In this book, I will try to show that the logic that links the destiny of human beings and chimpanzees is more than a convenient conceit. I look at the fortunes of chimps much as miners view the health of the songbirds they bring down into the shafts. The good fortune of chimps augurs well for us; their misfortune does not. The image of a truck rumbling off to a medical lab with chimpanzee veterans of sign-language experiments is far from reassuring.

During the past two years, I have spent some time catching up on the apes I first met fourteen years ago and have seen intermittently ever since. I have gone back to Oklahoma, where Washoe, Lucy, and many other chimps first made their gestures. I have visited LEMSIP, the medical laboratory where some of these chimps now live, and I have gone to Africa to see how well Lucy has adapted to the wild.

What I have seen has been disquieting, not only because of the tragic chemistry between human and chimp but also because of what I have been forced to perceive as the frail underpinnings of science and human judgments—including my own. The ebullience that greeted news that chimps had learned sign language is certainly gone. With few exceptions, the participants have been exhausted if not embittered by their experiences with sign-language experiments and the passions those experiments aroused. Few of them want to look back.

One of the curiosities of the past fifteen years has been a group of psychologists who have argued that the idea of the language capacity of apes is so preposterous that it should not be investigated at all. Instead of arguing that money should be spent either to prove or to put to rest the notion that man and ape share some cognitive-linguistic abilities, this group argues that the question has no scientific interest.

Given the polarization ape language experiments have caused in the behavioral sciences—one informal poll of

eminent psychologists found some saying that the fact
that chimps had learned to use a human language was the
most significant event of the past twenty-five years,
while another group claimed that the fact that chimps
had not learned to use language was the most significant
event of the past twenty-five years—it is little wonder
that the debate over what these experiments mean has
been stalled for fifteen years. Progress will come in this
debate only when theological questions are disentangled
from scientific questions, and I am not sure that in this
case they can be.

Having watched the events of these years, I find myself from time to time wondering if those pro-ignorance
scientists may not be right. Perhaps it would be better to
stick to figuring out the nature of stars and matter, and
not to concern ourselves with creatures who threaten to
paralyze us by shedding light on the true nature and origins of our abilities. Dismaying as this may sound, it is
quite possible that we cannot afford to know who we
are.

Fortunately there is another, less dour way of looking
at these events. While very little in the way of comparative language research is going on today, there is a veritable renaissance in the study of the cognitive behavior of
animals. Even scientists who ridicule the idea of continuity between animal and human language have enthusiastically endorsed continuities between man and animal in
other cognitive areas. Moreover, field researchers have
been taking a new look at the communication systems of
various animals. Some of this new work derives from or
was inspired by the original sign-language work with
chimps. While there are a few scientists who would
prefer that the work had never taken place, most of the
critics recognize that the language experiments have
provided a tantalizing window into a nonhuman intelligence. Thus it may be that the language-using chimps are
suffering the consequences of having shown themselves
before the world was ready to see them, and the scien-

tists who trained them, the disgrace of having a good idea before the world was ready for it.

Even as chimps like Ally languish in the medical lab, researchers inspired by their words of ten years ago pursue other lines of inquiry into the animal mind which further undermine the legal and ethical basis of their incarceration. Like a stone that initially causes a tiny but ultimately shattering crack in a windshield, the influence of the ape-language experiments continues to be felt through the behavioral sciences even as active interest in the direct study of ape language abilities dwindles.

This book will take note of the indirect influence of these experiments, but primarily it will be concerned with the life stories of a few chimps. In the long run, their fate may prove to be of far greater importance to the world than the debate over whether or not we share the gift of language with the great apes.

CHAPTER TWO

Signs of Discontent

I AM NOT a scientist; rather, I am an occasional observer of science. Some fourteen years ago, I became fascinated with the attempts to teach apes language, and my interest has led me to write three books and a number of articles about the subject. It all began with Washoe, a chimpanzee born in the wild and reared in captivity. Fourteen years ago, when I first met her, Washoe had already made her major contribution to science. Everything that is recounted in this book traces in some way back to Washoe, and so I shall start with her. And because it was Washoe's identity as the subject of the first successful attempt to establish two-way communication with an animal using a human language that gave such importance to her later extracurricular activities, I will deal with the scientific part of her life first.

Washoe (who is named after an Indian tribe that lived near Reno, Nevada, where she was raised) first became well-known when R. Allen Gardner and Beatrice Gardner, a husband and wife team of scientists, began publishing the details of her accomplishments in the years following her life as a scientific subject. Since the first full accounts of Washoe's use of American Sign Language (Ameslan) emerged in the early 1970s, she has been exhaustively written about in both the scientific and the popular press. The debate about the meaning of what Washoe did continues to this day. And so, in the next few pages, I will briefly summarize what the Gardners did with Washoe.

It all began with a flash of insight. Two scientists watching movies of an earlier failed attempt to teach a chimp spoken language noticed that the ape was intelligible when the sound track was turned off. The chimp was moving her lips into the proper shape but for some reason could not generate the appropriate sounds. The Gardners (his expertise was in verbal learning, hers in ethology, the biology of behavior) had the common sense to wonder whether the reason that chimps could not speak might be motor rather than mental. They went about structuring, analyzing, and writing about the experiment with equal common sense. The Gardners took their share of criticism over the years, some of it unfair, some of it deserved (Allen Gardner is a legendarily difficult man to deal with), but their initial work—carried out between 1966 and 1970—provides the bedrock of this field. Taken out of the context of the issues their work touched on, Project Washoe would seem routine, even pedestrian. But because the issues they were addressing were sensitive ones, everything about the project, from the Gardners' methods to their data, is fraught with drama and controversy.

Washoe was acquired by the Gardners when she was one year old. They chose to teach the chimp Ameslan because it was a widely used language and because it was gestural. (As noted, this is the language of the deaf in North America.) A word in Ameslan consists of a gesture made in a particular place in front of the body, with either one or both hands. The word for "hurt," for in-

stance, consists of repeatedly twisting together the tips of
the extended first fingers of each hand while the hands are
held in front of the chest. The key elements of a sign are the
place where the sign is made, the shaping of the hands, and
the movement. Word order—which over the past ten
years became such a bone of contention in the debate over
these experiments—does not have the significance that it
does in spoken language. It does tend to become regular-
ized with longer statements, but nearly all chimp statements in sign language are short, and in short statements,
many of the meanings served by word order in spoken
language can be conveyed through inflection and subtle
variations in the making of a sign.

One self-acknowledged deficiency of Project Washoe
was that it was not staffed by any native speakers of sign
language—a problem the Gardners addressed in subsequent experiments with other chimps.

The Gardners were conservative in what they would
consider a word in Ameslan. For instance, body parts
can be named by pointing to them in sign language.
While a number of subsequent experiments accepted
such actions as words, the Gardners did not include
signs consisting of pointing at body parts in Washoe's
reliable vocabulary.

With no precedents to guide them, the Gardners tried
a number of different methods to teach the ape to make
signs. The most productive method turned out to be
"molding," in which the teacher would actually shape
Washoe's hands into the appropriate configuration while
showing her an object or a picture of what the gesture
represented. The proposal to use molding was the contribution to Project Washoe of a young graduate student
named Roger Fouts. Discussion of various methods of
teaching the language formed the basis of his doctoral
dissertation.

Once Washoe's vocabulary began to grow, she acquired signs in a variety of different ways, ranging from
hands-on instruction to Washoe's observations of the

gestures people were making around her. Washoe also invented a few gestures on her own.

For a word to be considered a reliable part of her vocabulary, Washoe had to use it appropriately and spontaneously at least once a day for fifteen days. As her vocabulary grew, this required some unnatural situations since Washoe might not have cause to resort to the more exotic words in her vocabulary for fifteen consecutive days. (At different times critics have wondered whether some words described as spontaneous were in fact elicited, and whether there were any real controls over the people recording her utterances.) The experimenters also checked the reliability of her vocabulary periodically through what is called double-blind testing.

Double-blind testing is a somewhat cumbersome procedure which involves the person or animal to be tested and three testers. It gets its name because neither the person presenting a stimulus nor the person recording the answers can see what the person or animal being tested is responding to.

Washoe would be seated in front of the sliding door of a cabinet. One person, who could not see Washoe, would flash randomly arranged slides onto a screen in front of the ape when she opened the sliding door. Another person, who could not see the person flashing the slide, would ask Washoe in sign language what she saw and record Washoe's response. A third person in another room from the first observer and Washoe would also record her response through a one-way mirror. The second observer acted as a control on the accuracy of the first observer's interpretations of Washoe's responses.

The setup was designed to prevent the testers from unconsciously cuing Washoe. If the testers wanted to conspire to cheat consciously, there was little to stop them. No one has accused the experimenters of fraud of this magnitude (though one particularly vituperative critic keeps hinting at it). Rather, criticism has focused on unconscious and inadvertent leakage in the structure.

For instance, Carolyn Ristau and Donald Robbins, who did a thorough review of all language work done with apes, note the *possibility* (emphasis mine) that Washoe's nonverbal responses to objects might give a hint as to their meaning—i.e., getting excited when shown a banana—and that in general the items shown to her during a particular period were much smaller in number than her total vocabulary.

Another critic has suggested that the testers could inadvertently relay signals to each other that gave both the testers and Washoe an idea of what the appropriate response should be. This critic, Thomas Sebeok, carried out a lengthy examination of the Gardners' procedures, pointing out opportunities for the student to pick up cues to the right answers to the test or for the testers to determine the correct responses. For instance, "The Gardners report that 02 [the second observer] communicated his interpretations of Washoe's signs verbally, as they [02 and the projectionist] sat side by side, in which case how do we know that 01 [the first observer] could not hear 02's spoken observations, which might be expected to influence his own, thus leading to an increased degree of agreement between the two?"

On a couple of occasions, the Gardners used as an observer a stranger, unfamiliar with either Washoe or the experiment, but fluent in Ameslan. The presence of the naïve observer could not altogether have prevented unconscious cuing (if in fact it was possible) but it would have acted somewhat as a control against guessing.

In a perfect world with unlimited funding, an experimenter might be able to close all leakage in the testing procedure, but such a setup might in fact send cues of its own. One wonders, for instance, how a human infant would perform in a testing procedure in which strangers with fixed expressions or a disembodied computer-generated voice grilled the little boy or girl on vocabulary items. As it is now, babies tend not to do as well as chimps in highly structured testing situations.

By the third year, Washoe satisfied the requirements for reliability for 85 signs, which she used singly and in combinations (her reliable vocabulary rose to 132 signs after this). She asked questions, and she used the negative.

THIS, IN a nutshell, is what Washoe did. Her simple-seeming accomplishments caused quite a stir. Early reports of her achievements simultaneously prompted some anthropologists to speak of science's having to rethink what makes us human, and some linguists and psycholinguists to denigrate Project Washoe as ill conceived and unconvincing. Many of the early critics later mitigated their harshest criticisms as the Gardners published more and more of their results, but then a new wave of critics would appear, sometimes even citing a paper that had since been recanted by its author. Throughout these tumultuous times, it seemed that virtually everyone had lost sight of what language was, and in particular what sign language was.

This was not surprising because at the time there was no commonly accepted definition of language, and little was known about sign language. Today there still is no commonly accepted definition of language. However, the past decade has produced very fruitful studies of sign language. Ironically a number of the sign-language studies were spurred by Project Washoe, and one of the principal investigators of sign language has been Ursula Bellugi, one of the early dismissive critics of Washoe's achievements.

One criticism of the Gardners that has been voiced over the years goes to the heart of the maddening uncertainties that even today prevent any definite judgments about the language capacity of chimpanzees. The criticism is that the Gardners never understood chimps and never developed a relationship with them. Each of the scientists who have explored ape language has had to address a number of questions: What are an ape's needs? What is likely to motivate it to take part in the experiment? In answering these questions and in structuring experiments, the scientists reveal their assumptions about the nature of learning, the nature of apes, and the nature of language.

Some of the scientists investigating ape language capacity attempted to limit personal contact with the animals and to reduce language to a set of problems the chimps had to solve. Others felt that since language is essentially communication, the stronger the relationship between scientist and ape, the more likely the experiment to succeed. Thus, the era was dotted with experiments that either produced credible-looking data on something that bore little resemblance to language, or else produced behaviors very much like language use but which were suspect because of the relationship of scientist and animal. There have been elements of both in Washoe's long career in sign language.

Project Washoe was the first of a large number of attempts to teach language to the great apes. Most of those attempts involved American Sign Language, but two others (which I will not be discussing in this book) involved invented languages. A scientist named David Premack attempted to teach a chimp named Sarah to construct sentences using a language in which the words consisted of plastic tokens at roughly the same time the Gardners began work with Washoe. In the early 1970s, Duane Rumbaugh began exploring the potential of communicating with chimps through computers using a language designed by linguist Erich Van Glasersfeld.

Over the years Project Washoe has become a useful test to determine attitudes toward sign-language experiments. While there has always been a good deal of bickering within the field about what might be the most productive way to proceed in the investigation of language, attitudes toward Project Washoe seem to reflect attitudes toward language work with chimps in general.

Those unwilling to accept that Washoe learned words and used them in productive ways generally feel that there is no evidence that any chimp in any experiment ever demonstrated anything remotely like language use. While I have met people who feel that other scientists, such as Duane and Sue Savage-Rumbaugh or David Premack, had more interesting experiments, I have yet to meet a critic who rejects Project Washoe as proof that chimps can learn words but still accepts one of the other experiments as demonstrating chimp capacity for language. On the other hand, those who believe that Washoe did learn words and use them in productive ways might well prefer other experiments as more interesting explorations of aspects of language.

Did or did not Washoe use language? The question is really unanswerable until science decides what language is. In the meantime, for fifteen years the jury of scientific opinion has swayed back and forth on the question. For the apes involved these swings of opinion were of more than academic interest. At first, there was only good news for the chimps involved.

CHAPTER THREE

Heady Days

IT WAS by way of Vietnam that I got involved in writing about experiments that attempted to impart language to chimpanzees. In 1971, I was in Southern California. I was not long out of college, and I had given myself six weeks to prove that I could earn a living as a writer. I had gone to California because I had an introduction to an editor of the *Los Angeles Times*. This produced a commission to write an article about the role of fads in the rock music scene for their Sunday magazine. This first commission gave me a rather shaky start. The *Los Angeles Times* didn't like what I wrote, but with the minuscule payment the *Times* gave me, I could at least argue that I should keep trying to write. (Years later the article saw the light of day as part of one of my books.) It was during this visit to California that I first heard about language experiments with chimpanzees.

One evening, I found myself at a small get-together in Irvine, California. I ended up talking to a linguistics professor from the nearby University of California. The man casually mentioned that "someone up the coast was trying to teach an invented language to a chimpanzee." (He was referring to David Premack's experiment with plastic tokens.) Keep in mind that this was California in the early 1970s, where someone at a cocktail party might also casually mention that he had just returned from an astral body voyage to Saturn. In general, I would try to keep a neutral face when hearing things like this, but in this case the remark was coming from a very sober-minded professor, and for me it was like a bolt of lightning. Still somewhat naïve about the nature of journalism, I thought the world would be fascinated by a question that has dogged philosophy for centuries: namely, what is the difference between man and animal? It was because I tended to become fascinated with issues like this that I was having such a hard time getting started as a writer. Though impractical, I was still realistic enough to understand that as an unknown twenty-three-year-old, I had little chance of finding an organization to finance an investigation of *any* project I might want to undertake, much less a look at attempts to impart language to other animals. A year later, things were a little different.

In the interim, I had gained some attention for an article I had written about fragging in Vietnam. Fragging was a sad, violent by-product of the demoralization of our army in Vietnam. The word referred to attacks by enlisted men on the noncoms and officers above them. I was asked by a publisher whether I would like to expand my article into a book. I declined, but I took the invitation as an opportunity to broach the idea of writing a book about the attempts to teach language to other animals and the implications of those attempts.

After several months of research, I made my first trip to Oklahoma to visit the Institute for Primate Studies. Madelaine and I drove out West in a camper borrowed from my parents and plunked ourselves in a campground a few miles from the institute.

The Institute for Primate Studies had been established by William Lemmon, a clinical psychologist, as a place to study maternal and sexual behavior. It was loosely affiliated with the University of Oklahoma. Lemmon, a Buddha-shaped man, had started by studying sheep and gradually moved on to the study of primates. In the process he converted his farm into a home for gibbons, siamangs, various monkeys, peacocks, and livestock, as well as chimpanzees. The chimps were housed in a series of interconnected cages that erupted through the roof of an elaborate pink plaster structure connected by a breezeway to Lemmon's house. Not far away Lemmon had installed another colony of chimps on one of two islands he had created in a small pond. Tall trees bordered the pond, and gibbons arced gracefully through the branches of trees on the other island. However, the chimps had virtually denuded their island of foliage and had to make do with climbing poles placed there for their exercise.

Throughout the compound pleasant, purposeful-looking students and keepers went about their tasks. The countryside surrounding the institute is undulating and veldtlike. If one ignored the barrenness of the chimp island, which offered a plangent note of ugliness, the place looked like a little paradise.

I made this first trip in 1972, and it was an exciting time for the ape language experiments and the Institute for Primate Studies. Roger Fouts had come to Oklahoma a year earlier from Reno, Nevada. He was accompanied by Washoe. Fouts was soon to be awarded a PhD for his work assisting on Project Washoe.

In another era, Roger Fouts probably would not have gone into academia at all. He came from California, where he had a typical early sixties Southern Californian upbringing of football, cars, and girls. He started out at a junior college, got a master's from Long Beach State, and worked in a bank before going to the University of Nevada at Reno for graduate work in psychology. There he met the Gardners and Washoe, and suddenly his life had a definite direction. He discovered that he had a gift for relating to chimpanzees. Since then, Washoe has been a continuously dominant figure in his life.

When I met Roger, he was brimming with ideas about the directions he wanted to pursue in his research, and brimming with enthusiasm about the prospects for success. He also managed to impart that enthusiasm to the cadre of graduate and undergraduate assistants who came to Oklahoma to be part of this brave new world in which animals might talk to people. Roger talked about setting up a project in which he would install a population of sign-language-using chimps on fifty acres and create a situation that would encourage cooperative behavior and perhaps a primitive economic system. "Chimps understand money as well as we do," Roger said back then.

To a degree, the ape language experiments were a product of their times. It is more than coincidence that when much of the nation was either rethinking or rebelling against the political, economic, environmental, and corporate assumptions that had dominated American life, scientists also began to question the assumptions that governed the behavioral sciences. The ethos that looked for continuity rather than discontinuity between man and animal was very much in concord with the pantheistic feelings that gripped the imagination of my generation.

That the experiments were a product of their times was to have negative repercussions later on. When the mood is with you—and it must be said that in the early 1970s there was a constituency fully prepared to believe that chimps were capable of language no matter what the evidence mustered for or against the contention—the temptation is to be less rigorous than one might be in a universally hostile environment. To be sure, the behavioral sciences were hostile to the experiments, but the critics were largely the old guard, while the young scientists pursuing this work were buoyed by the knowledge that many of their younger peers shared their vision of our place in nature.

Apart from the tenor of the times, it is a formidable experience to watch for the first time as a chimpanzee converses using sign language. A number of critics who scorned reports of chimps using sign language had on-the-spot conversions after watching the animals use the language in interchanges with people. You watch the give and take, the facial expressions, the verbal tics, etc., that the chimp makes as it tries to get its meaning across, and you *know* that something more than rote learning is going on. But it is exasperatingly hard to pin down in words and data.

That first day of my visit, Washoe was temporarily housed in a metal holding cage until she could rejoin the other chimps on the island in the pond. She was outraged with her quarters, and she let everybody know with a variety of chimp and human expressions. The chimp vocalizations were a series of hoots that turned into screams. Washoe would intersperse these impressive noises with a series of gestures denoting that she wanted food, or to be let out. Getting no response, she made another series of gestures, this time patting the underside of her chin with the top of her flattened hand before signing the handler's name. This new sign meant "dirty," a word she seemed to be using to convey an opinion rather than to describe a condition.

It is pretty heady stuff to see something like that. And it must have been frustrating for Roger Fouts to observe such things day in and day out and then read accounts by people who had never visited Washoe which claimed that what Washoe was displaying was reward-inspired imitation no different than that displayed by a trained pigeon. On the contrary, it was quite clear that Washoe was trying to communicate, frantically at times, with the people who occasionally walked by. Whether she was using language is another question.

The first day Madelaine and I went to the institute, we

also met two young chimps who were gamboling around the farmyard, terrorizing the peacocks and any other animal they thought they might intimidate. Their names were Booee and Bruno, and they were just beginning to learn signs at that time. Roger Fouts hoped to use them in an ambitious—never-to-be-realized—experiment involving a free-roaming, language-using chimp colony. Booee had had a sad history before coming to the institute. He had been born at the National Institutes of Health near Washington, D.C., and early in life had been part of an experiment to study the effects of severing the corpus callosum, which connects the two halves of the brain. At this point, though, he showed few ill effects of his earlier life in the lab. I got into the fun and played with Bruno and Booee for a bit. Bruno would climb up onto a tractor seat and leap off onto me over and over again. After a while, a young male chimp inevitably begins to test you, and it is a little unsettling to be confronted with an animal who does not automatically acknowledge your paramountcy in the natural hierarchy.

A little later that day, I went back over to Washoe's cage with Roger, and at his approach she quieted. "You can't blame her for feeling slighted," he said as he opened the cage to let her out. Back then I was struck by the bond between Roger and Washoe, though I did not really know how passionately Roger was devoted to chimps, particularly Washoe. (The depth of that passion did not really become apparent until years later, when Washoe came under attack.)

Roger Fouts believed that a strong relationship with a chimpanzee is necessary in order to study communication with the animal. And it was evident from my first session with him and Washoe together that he was devoted to chimpanzees, and to Washoe in particular. Chimps are immensely strong and, as they get older, sometimes unpredictable, but Roger seemed to understand the moods of the chimps at the institute and how to deal with them. To Roger they were people. Thelma was lazy; Cindy, a "dreamer"; Bruno, "proud"; Booee, "a chimp willing to sell his soul for a raisin." It is hard to say what it is about Roger that was the basis of his rapport with the animals. He can be calm, but he also can be quite excitable. He claimed that it was his consistent assertion of dominance, but that did not seem to be the case either. One associate, Chris O'Sullivan, contrasted Lemmon and Fouts this way: "Roger had a way with chimps, but Lemmon had dominance."

Roger's rapport defies obvious explanation, but it is nonetheless real. By all accounts, Roger is truly gifted in dealing with chimps. A former associate, George Kimball, says, "Roger is the best I've ever seen at working with chimps." According to Kimball, one key to Roger's gift is the ability to assume a posture of righteous indignation—"How dare you do that!"—something Kimball feels the chimps understand.

I thought back then that had he not decided that he wanted to be a scientist, Roger Fouts might make a comfortable living as a trainer—something he has in fact done from time to time in recent years.

That first day my attention was on Washoe, and, a little nervous about meeting a full-grown chimp for the first time, I was grateful for whatever relationship Roger might have with the animal. Washoe gave Roger a big hug when she came out, and then we went for a walk.

During the walk, Roger picked up an apple and offered it to Washoe, signing, "What's this?" Washoe knuckle-walked over to us from the tree in which she had been playing and made the sign for "fruit" by placing her fist against the side of her mouth. Roger asked her, "Who fruit?" to which she replied, "Washoe fruit." Roger said, "What Washoe fruit?" and Washoe dutifully said, "Please Washoe fruit."

Depending on who you talk to, this was either a conversation, or, on Washoe's part at least, a rote response triggered by the opportunity to get a reward, or a rote behavior cued either consciously or unconsciously by

Roger, or a series of hand movements only vaguely associated in Washoe's mind with the symbols and sentences Roger thought he was eliciting. It is also a dead ringer for innumerable conversations Madelaine and I have recently had with our daughter, Gillian.

It did not take an experience with a child of our own to realize how strongly language is bound up with the relationship between the speakers, but looking at it as a scientific proposition, we would have a hopeless time proving that Gillian had any language at all. The infant who at nineteen months could recite from memory "Baa Baa, Black Sheep" from beginning to end would clam up if asked to perform for friends, or would recite the first verse over and over. Ordinary discourse was characterized on our part by shameless cuing, outright prompting, and dubious interpretations of Gillian's gnomic, if not unintelligible, utterances. In fact, at eighteen months, Gillian began to demonstrate most of the behaviors critics have cited as evidence that apes cannot learn language: she interrupted, she repeated phrases incessantly, she responded inappropriately, and she jumbled her word order.

Of course, as the months went on, Gillian got a better grip on things and later surpassed any ape I have observed in the explicitness, richness, and complexity of her utterances. The question is, what was going on at those points at which there appeared to be such an overlap between chimp and child?

Back in 1972 no one knew the answer to that question, and even today it is doubtful that any experiment has been sufficiently well designed to determine at what point an ape reaches its limits in language acquisition. Different experiments established a number of ways in which apes understand and use words, but the demands of studying more complex aspects of language proved to be beyond the resources of those involved in the work. Moreover, given the persistent disagreements that have mired discussion for fifteen years, it would have been hard to marshal the support necessary to find funding for a more ambitious language undertaking. (The Rumbaughs have had great success recently raising money, but their research has turned away from language and toward other cognitive capacities.)

In retrospect the interesting, if maddeningly inconclusive, results with regard to more complex uses of language came from experiments in which the ape had a relationship with the experimenter—experiments in which the use of the language was a natural part of the animal's day and its commerce with its cohorts. It was from such experiments that the most extravagant claims for ape language use came—experiments with the fewest controls and the most passionately committed experimenters. Thus we had a situation bred perfectly for the most vituperative type of debate.

I can see now that despite the outward appearance of paradisal harmony that first day at the Institute for Primate Studies, the seeds of a vast, sometimes violent discord were apparent in this unlikely cooperative venture of man and animal. Perhaps I should have been more attuned to the disquieting image of the denuded chimp island.

The relative freedom with which Roger let the chimps mingle with humans was to redound negatively years later; the absence from the scene of William Lemmon portended a conflict that was ultimately to bring all language experimentation to a halt at the institute; the passionate loyalty of Roger to his nonhuman colleagues was ultimately to raise suspicions about the validity of the claims he was to make over the years about the things his chimps said and did; the presence of leashes and cattle prods provided intimations that the relationship of man and chimp is not an easy fit. And finally there was a question that occurred to me then and which has not gone away in the fourteen years during which I have been observing and thinking about this work: What about the chimps? What does this all mean from their

point of view? How much faith should they have had in
the lavish expressions of everlasting loyalty voiced by
those attempting to erase the barriers that categorized
the chimps among the dumb beasts, without rights, without a soul?

Washoe, Booee, Bruno, Ally, and all the other chimps
in other experiments did not elect to join these experiments. Strangers in a strange land, they were prey to the
vicissitudes of fashion, funding, and fickle human sym-
pathies. A chimp might live longer than forty years, and
all these chimps were young. For the moment they were
a hot item, indeed a meal ticket of sorts, but would the
attention of their human sponsors outlast their funding
and their vogue? With a few exceptions it would not.

As the apes matured, their relationships with people
changed, and as the relationships changed, those
changes affected communication between human and
ape. And these changes affected the study of communication.

For the apes in these studies, these changes were not
a casual matter. In the case of every one of these animals, the relationship between the experimenter and the
animal had figured critically in the quality of the ape's
life, and in the likely duration of the ape's life once the
language experiments began to wind down.

CHAPTER FOUR

Personae

A DETECTIVE looking into the chimp movements that followed the end of the language experiments might ask, "Where's the money? Where are the human entanglements?" He would be on the right track. This is not to say that any of the people involved loved the chimps less, but rather that *human* movements to a large degree determined chimp movements, and the human movements were governed as much by the flux of human relationships as anything else. And so before getting into chimp-to-human relationships, it is useful to understand the key human-to-human tension that was at work at the Institute for Primate Studies.

For both the chimps and the people at the Institute for Primate Studies, William Lemmon was the dominant figure. He had started the institute, and though his charisma was not immediately apparent to an outsider, he had an influence over both students and faculty at the university that went beyond anything that might be credited to his scientific reputation.

The power Lemmon exercised over his colleagues

and patients is evident from passages in a book written by Maurice Temerlin, a former student and patient of Lemmon's. Though the book, *Lucy, Growing Up Human*, is about Lucy, a chimpanzee the Temerlins raised, Temerlin spends a good deal of time writing about Lemmon (identified in the book only as the "therapist"), with whom his life was deeply entangled: "I saw him as infallible, and I literally believed his most outlandish statements. I saw him as benevolent, and I ignored the most obvious evidence of human self-seeking and petti- ness. I saw him as omnipotent, and I was blind to his dependence on people who were dependent upon him. It was a horrible cosmic joke that out of unconscious needs for a God I selected a therapist who had unconscious needs to be worshipped."

Lemmon's ability to dominate situations was under- scored at various times when chimps broke out of the main cage complex. On one occasion, Lemmon report- edly called the local dogcatcher and asked him to round up the chimps. When the man wisely said, "No way," Lemmon went after the chimps himself and managed to bully the big males back into the cages. This is some- thing that no one else at the institute—including Roger Fouts—would have been able to pull off. In fact, when an adult female named Candy broke out, Roger backed off toward water (chimps cannot swim) and let Lemmon get her back into her cage.

In other ways, however, Roger Fouts was a serious threat to Dr. Lemmon. Although when he arrived he had not yet been awarded his PhD, Roger still came to Okla- homa invested with the dazzling allure of Washoe's achievements. Roger thus had a celebrity in the eyes of undergraduate and graduate students alike which Lem- mon could not make his own and which insulated Roger from Lemmon's control. One former graduate student described their relationship as "like two alpha [domi- nant] male chimps butting heads."

Time and again through the years, the tension between Roger and Lemmon would surface, sometimes trivially, sometimes seriously. As we shall see, other human relationships also figured in the chimps' destinies. I mention Fouts and Lemmon here because it is useful to keep their relationship in mind when considering Roger's relationship with Washoe.

Washoe

ALTHOUGH Washoe is best known for the facility with words that she demonstrated under the tutelage of the Gardners, ironically her tenure with them as an experimental subject was relatively brief in comparison with the time that she has since spent with Roger Fouts. Basically she has been the dominant figure in Fouts's life since they both left Reno, Nevada, for Oklahoma. She has determined his career choices and his living arrangements for more than fifteen years. While Roger has been away from Washoe for substantial periods during that time, he still has had to manage her life from afar.

Roger is also utterly devoted to Washoe. The way he feels about her is perhaps best revealed by an anecdote Roger recently recounted in the "Friends of Washoe" newsletter:

Several years ago, when Washoe was about seven or eight years old, I witnessed an event that told about Washoe as a person, as well as causing me to reflect on human nature. [The account proceeds to describe the chimp island at the institute] ...One day a young female by the name of Cindy could not resist the temptation of the mainland and jumped over the electric fence in an attempt to leap the moat. She hit the water with a great splash which caught my attention. I started running toward the moat intent on diving in to save her. As I approached I saw Washoe running toward the electric fence. Cindy had come to the surface, thrashing and submerging again. Then I witnessed Washoe jumping the electric fence and landing next to the fence on about a foot of bank. She then held on to the grass at the water's edge and stepped out onto the slippery mud underneath the water's surface. With the reach of her long arm, she grasped one of Cindy's flailing arms as she resurfaced and pulled her to the safety of the bank.... Washoe's act gave me a new perspective on chimpanzees. I was impressed with her heroism in risking her life on the slippery banks. She cared about someone in trouble; someone she didn't even know that well.

This little story shows that Roger's affection for Washoe goes beyond the interest a scientist might take in an experimental subject.

During the time Roger has worked with Washoe, he has used her in a number of experiments, but nothing she has done in language subsequent to leaving Reno has supplanted what she did during her childhood there. It's not that she stopped using words but rather that, since Reno, she has not studied in a strictly controlled setting. Moreover, with the debate over Washoe's abilities still mired in the basics, it is hard to get people to focus seriously on the more ambiguous issues Fouts has been exploring. Fouts is quite frank about his reasons for abandoning highly structured situations. He was constantly frustrated by the fact that, looking for one thing, he would see the chimps demonstrating something more interesting and yet entirely outside the experimental design. Consequently he now sees himself more as a reporter who tries to record what Washoe and her friends are doing.

The somewhat ironic result of all this is that Washoe, who was taken very seriously when under the instruction of the Gardners, is now taken less seriously, not because of what she is or is not doing, but because of the circumstances in which she is doing it. During the last few years it has been Washoe's behavior as a chimp, not as the subject of an experiment, that has received the most attention.

Chimps, like any other infrequently encountered species or group, tend to look alike and seem to act alike to us until we spend some time with them. We tend to think of them as interchangeable, as not having marked personality differences. But of course they do, and people who work with chimps form strong opinions about particular animals. To Roger, Washoe was never anything other than a devoted companion. To me, her personality was obscured at first by the noumena of her status as a chimp using sign language. For those who work with the animals, though, the chimps very quickly lose the distinction conferred upon them by their ability to make signs. The graduate students and caretakers who deal with them formed opinions based not on the animal's performance so much as on its temperament. At the Institute for Primate Studies, Ally was regarded as something of a nut, Booee as sweet, and Washoe, by some at least, as bad news, although this was an opinion that formed over a period of time. Ultimately the division of opinion about Washoe and her actions was to cause a profound rift at the institute.

Over the years, Washoe had to put up with different styles as well as different people. She did not see another chimp until she was brought to Oklahoma. When asked what they were, at one point she signed, "Black bug." Prior to Oklahoma, Washoe was spoiled excessively, but in Norman she found her status had dropped dramatically. She lost most of her human attendants, and she was thrown in with the "black bugs." From her exile she often and loudly proclaimed in sign language that she would rather be with people. Despite the devotion of Roger, Washoe had to accept a continual, progressive downgrading of her freedom and her status.

Lucy

THOUGH Roger had great plans for Washoe at Oklahoma, he gained more fame for his work with a chimp named Lucy. Lucy was a captive-born chimp who was being reared as part of a human family by Maurice and Jane Temerlin. Although Lucy was not at the Institute for Primate Studies, Dr. Lemmon, as noted earlier, was deeply entangled with her life.

The Temerlins lived in an affluent neighborhood in Norman, Oklahoma, in a house built and financed by William Lemmon. For much of Lucy's early life, Jane Temerlin worked at the Institute for Primate Studies. Ultimately both Maury and Jane severed their ties with Lemmon, and this split had consequences for Lucy.

However, during her first eleven years, Lucy lived the life of Riley in an attractive rambling ranch house bordered by an expanse of lawns and gardens. The Temerlins' teen-aged son, Steve, was there as a companion and sibling. At one point Lucy even had a pet cat. Her standard of living was considerably higher than that of many of the people who worked with her (or wrote about her). Her language studies began relatively late—when she was five—but she had Roger Fouts as a teacher and the accrued benefits of his experience in working with Washoe.

In concert with Roger Mellgren, a colleague in the psychology department at the University of Oklahoma, Roger studied Lucy's ability to use reliable signs to describe novel objects for which she had no word in her vocabulary of signs. After she had had two years of language instruction, Lucy's vocabulary rose to about seventy-five signs. What Fouts and Mellgren did was to present Lucy with twenty-four different fruits and vegetables, occasionally mixed with nonfood items for which she had a sign. The specific purpose of the experiment was to determine whether newly acquired words would become generic to the category of things she was shown or remain specific to only one of them. For instance, she was taught the sign for "berry" to refer first to cherries, and then, a few days later, to refer to blueberries. "Berry" did not stick in Lucy's mind as the sign for blueberries, but it did for cherries, from which the experimenters inferred that Lucy would rather use the sign in a specific sense. But perhaps the most interesting finding of the experiment was a sidelight to its main purpose.

When presented with a novel object, Lucy would sometimes create new combinations of signs to describe it. She called watermelon "candy drink" or "drink fruit" (Lucy did not have signs for "water" or "melon"). She referred to four different citrus fruits as "smell fruits," and after biting into a radish, which she did not like, she called it a "cry hurt food."

You can make a good deal of this, as well as of similar combinations used by other apes to describe novel objects. One simple thing this indicates is that the chimp's vocabulary was very much a part of the animal's life. Apart from Washoe, Lucy was more deeply immersed in sign language than any other ape in Norman.

I visited Lucy on several different occasions both during that first trip to Oklahoma and on subsequent trips. She clearly showed the benefits of the "enriched" environment in which she had grown up. She continually resorted to her vocabulary both to amuse herself and to relate to other people. When she first met me, she gave me a minute head to foot examination and, discovering a scab on my knee, touched the ends of her first fingers together repeatedly, which is the sign for "hurt."

Lucy was particularly interested in the little alligator insignia on my tennis shirt. She pointed to it several times and, looking at me, traced a question mark in the air. She was asking me what it was. Coached by Roger, I placed the heel of my hands together and made a snapping motion, an impromptu sign for "alligator." Lucy tried to imitate the sign but made it with the snapping motion originating from the tips of her fingers. The next day I showed up wearing a shirt of a different color but with the same insignia. Asked who I was, Lucy responded with the snapping sign, again originating from the tips of her fingers. Perhaps to Lucy it seemed that I was an "alligator."

Unlike a lot of other chimps whose signing was fast, almost frantic, Lucy used what might be described as the sign-language equivalent of a drawl in making gestures. One of her amusements was to play with her toys and sign to them, much in the fashion that human infants talk to their dolls.

As in the case of Washoe, a good deal has been written about Lucy and her use of language. I mention it here to stress the degree to which sign language was a part of Lucy's life in Oklahoma. This has some bearing on what happened to Lucy after experimentation was over.

With perhaps the exception of a gorilla named Koko (whom I will be dealing with later), Lucy suffered the fewest dislocations of any ape involved in the experiments with language. She grew up knowing she was different from humans; nevertheless, she had a means of communication through which she could make her wants and moods known to her human friends and family, and there was always someone to talk to. If not Roger or the Temerlins, a graduate student from the university would be there to provide companionship.

Ally

APART from Washoe and Lucy, the chimp at the institute who made the strongest impression on me was Ally. He was very bright, a very good signer, and he was also very agreeable. Like Lucy, he spent his early years as part of a household where, apart from learning sign language, he was apparently also given lessons in religion. One sign in Ally's vocabulary when I knew him was a crosslike sign that was supposed to signify Jesus. Ally was first used in a study using spoken English to teach sign language and vice versa.

When he was four, his foster mother got married and returned Ally to the Institute for Primate Studies. Since Ally had been with this woman since he was a few days old, the separation was traumatic, and he developed hysterical paralysis in one of his arms. Added to his problems was the hazing he suffered from his fellow chimps when he first arrived on the chimp island at the institute.

George Kimball began to work with Ally in a study of chimp use of prepositions, and Ally seized on George as a substitute for his lost mother. They developed a very strong relationship, which allowed George to take Ally outside even after he had grown into a big bruiser of a chimp.

Later on, after work with sign-language studies began to abate, Ally turned out to be a good breeder. He was always an extremely beguiling chimp. George said one reason he trusted himself to take Ally out as an adult male was that Ally seemed to be able to think ahead and realize that if he misbehaved, he might not be taken out again.

There were other celebrated ape language students in the early 1970s, but only two more that I came to know personally.

Nim

NIM, WHO was born at the Institute for Primate Studies, became a pupil of Herb Terrace in a sign-language project affiliated with the psychology department of Columbia University. Next to Washoe, Nim has received more public attention than any other chimp, not because of his achievements with language but because of what he supposedly did not do. Herbert Terrace's analysis of Nim's performance has led him to the conclusion that none of the signing chimps is doing much more than "running on with its hands until it gets what it wants." As we shall see, because of this judgment, Nim has had some impact on the lives of his chimpanzee peers.

Terrace's study of Nim focused on his use of words in combinations. Apart from one photo which graced an article in *New York Magazine* and which showed Nim and Terrace together taking a shower, Nim's relations with his master were relatively Victorian and remote. The experiment was characterized by a highly structured teaching and testing situation, and during the course of less than four years, Nim had sixty different trainers. With a year of funding remaining, Terrace returned Nim to the Institute for Primate Studies, where he languished for some years. The Nim that returned to the institute was somewhat different from before—easily intimidated by the females of the chimp colony and prone to biting humans. But this was not the last we were to hear of Nim. He was to reenter the headlines as a central figure in the cause célèbre that centered on the dispersal of the chimp colony in 1982.

Koko

ONE OTHER ape became something of a celebrity in the language experiments of the 1970s. This was Koko, a lowland gorilla. Raised from infancy by Penny Patterson,

Koko has the longest tenure of any ape in a continuous sign-language experiment. Penny Patterson has been involved with Koko since the very outset of her graduate career at Stanford University. She is also very well known to the outside world. This young blonde woman, who habitually wears a blue laboratory coat, is probably one of the more recognizable people in the behavioral sciences.

Penny has claimed at various times that Koko has used language to swear, joke, and lie (uses of language that have been attributed to some signing chimps), but also to rhyme, and even that she has demonstrated an understanding of spelling. As coauthor with Penny Patterson of the book *The Education of Koko*, I had the opportunity to spend a good deal of time with Koko, and my impression is that she has integrated sign language into her life to a remarkable extent, more so than any sign-language-using chimp I have been exposed to.

It is very easy to like a gorilla, even a somewhat spoiled one like Koko. They are of course large, but also, I feel, generous-spirited. Koko really enjoys a good joke, even if it is at her expense. Gorillas are much less excitable than chimpanzees, and Koko's signing was much more clear and precise than that of the chimpanzees I observed.

Penny suffers from a credibility problem not unlike that which bedevils Roger Fouts. Both are suspect because of the passion with which they defend their animals. Unlike Roger, Penny plays things very close to the vest, limiting visits by outside observers, as well as access to her raw data. Since 1978 she has had no affiliation with any university, or any government funding agency. She has gradually built a little kingdom for herself and her gorillas in a secluded spot in Woodside, California. She raises money to support her work through a newsletter and private donations. While these keep her going, her reputation suffers because her proprietary behavior lends a sinister connotation to her lone wolf status.

Still, Penny is utterly devoted to Koko and to a young male gorilla named Michael. More than any other person in this work, Penny has, so far, given over her life to her ape.

Growing Up
Chimpanzee in America

THESE, then, are the ape dramatis personae. Although each of the various experiments mentioned so far has followed a different course, two threads have run through all of them, radically affecting the course of the experiment: the first is the relationship of the experimenter and the animal, and the second is the way in which the world has viewed the results (to be discussed in later chapters). Quite simply, the animals grew up, and as they grew up, the people in contact with them discovered that they were neither domestic animals nor people. Their great strength necessitated restrictions on their freedom; at a point in which the animals were maturing and therefore eager to explore their world, they would find their periods of freedom decreasing. The freedom to roam through a private house would be replaced by confinement in various forms of cages. Trips outside their cages would become more and more infrequent, and on those rare occasions, the ape would have to suffer the indignity of a leash.

There were long periods when not even Roger would take Washoe out. And when I visited them in the mid-1970s, I noticed that Roger was visibly more on edge when we went for a walk than he had been during my first visit five years earlier.

The sensitive animals could not help but notice the fear and nervousness that they could inspire in the peripheral people in their lives. Although they have rarely turned on those they perceive to be their foster family, they are not above taking advantage of their capacity to terrify others. And this in turn leads to further restraints upon them, until the life of the adult ape differs only slightly from the life of a chimp in a well-run zoo.

This progression cannot help but affect the relationship between the animal and its foster family—"Why are you locking me up? Why is everybody so nervous? Why must we communicate through bars?"—and this in turn cannot help but affect the communication between human being and ape, no matter what medium is being used.

It used to be said that the greatest difficulty that arose in the study of the language capacities of dolphins was that the animals spent 98 percent of their time below water, while people spent 98 percent of their time above water. In a certain sense, the ape language experiments suffer from the same difficulty. The only time when the chimp might feel that it is a natural, integrated part of a human family is during the first three years of life. Beyond that age, its strength and willfulness—and therefore its ability to do substantial physical harm to people —cause its keepers to shrink from the prospect of liability suits if not from the animal itself. At that point, obviously, the situation is not natural at all.

It is possible for people to have relationships with adult, free-roaming chimpanzees for a large number of years in unconstrained circumstances, but it is improbable that it could be done in the United States. Apart from the logistical and legal difficulties, there is the question of how many people could bear up under the stress of fulfilling the needs of these energetic and insatiably demanding animals. Spending a week with a four-year-old male chimp is like spending a month with a hyperactive six-year-old with the strength of an NFL lineman.

All these factors have an erosive effect on the perception that some sort of authentic familial bond connects a particular chimp and a particular human being, and this in turn has an effect on the nature and substance of the communication taking place between them.

As I renewed contacts with various people in the ape language experiments, I was struck by the change of mood that has emerged over a period of years. The sunny optimism that seemed to characterize the Institute for Primate Studies on my first visit had given way to doubt; conflicts had begun to appear among the experimenters, conflicts which ultimately led to the dissolution of the chimp colony.

Before turning to an examination of these conflicts, I should explore an event that occurred at the very moment when energies were seen to flag among the proponents of these experiments. It was a situation that called to mind Yeats' lines "The best lack all conviction, while the worst Are full of passionate intensity."

CHAPTER FIVE

The Quagmire

As IN THE case of so many college offices, the doors of Everett Dale Hall at the University of Oklahoma are bedecked with cartoons and aphorisms. Roger Fouts occupied room 736. Amid the mosaic of paper stuck to his door were two quotes, printed together on a slip of paper: "Up yours, you jive turkey"—the utterance of a myna bird at a Texaco station on Highway 9, between Battle Creek and Detroit—and "Baby in my drink"—a sign-language exclamation by Washoe. The proximity of those two quotes on Roger's door had the effect back in the 1970s of underscoring the difference between a bird's mimicry and Washoe's ability to describe something that had actually happened—the misfortune of a toy doll falling into her glass of water. In the late 1970s, when I used this anecdote to open an article about the language experiments, the irony was clear to anyone who read the newspapers. Today, because of the ministrations of many critics, a number of people might feel that both statements were indistinguishably meaningless. In fact, Herb Terrace, once involved in sign-language experimentation but now its most energetic critic, has argued as much with reference to Washoe's exclamation quoted above.

In contrast to the general ebullience manifest during my first visit to the Institute for Primate Studies, the situation during the last few years has been a gloomy one. The futility and vituperation of the past decade have so demoralized those previously involved with the work that the few people who are still investigating language capacities of apes prefer to bill their work as something else in order to enhance the possibilities of funding. A few years back Duane and Sue Savage-Rumbaugh wrote, "Frankly we are not interested in whether or not language is the exclusive domain of man. That question leads all who address it to a quagmire of confusion, despair and impatience. We want none of that!" This is a sentiment that might be echoed by many other people who find themselves perpetually arguing over basics.

However, similar statements by other scientists have been misunderstood to mean that the individuals involved have repudiated their earlier beliefs with respect to the question of continuity between animal and human communication. With a couple of notable exceptions, the facts are otherwise. Or, rather, the bottomless ambiguity of the question makes it impossible to address within the framework of any ordinary experimental design. It is as though a client commissioned an architect to build a structure but could not decide whether he wanted the structure to be a tent or a house or an office building.

It is my feeling that the ascendancy of what might be called the negative view of ape language experiments followed not so much from any clear-cut reading of the data as from a loss of energy and heart among the proponents who had to contend with these ambiguities. Irrespective of the merits of an idea, a passionate advocate can promote a theory long after it has ceased to have any utility. (Witness Noam Chomsky, who has managed to keep the foundering ship of deep structure afloat for two decades principally through his intimidating brilliance and his willingness to debate anyone anywhere who challenges his ideas.) On the other hand, no matter how well grounded or appropriate an idea or theory, it is unlikely to persist without champions. This is particularly true if the idea challenges an entrenched establishment with a deep personal commitment to another theory. There is nothing inevitable about truth in science, particularly if truth is not about the nature of matter but about a variously defined phenomenon called language.

PERHAPS the best way to characterize the "quagmire" which the debate over ape language abilities has become is to note that nineteen years after Washoe said her first words, there is still active discussion in learned journals about what those first words mean. In the interim, there have been dozens of different experiments with some thirty-odd apes, and there are even a few experiments still going on today; nevertheless, there is no consensus on the basics—namely Project Washoe—that might allow the scientific community to turn its attention toward these other results. One can't make a judgment about Koko or Nim or Lucy or Lana or any of the others without looking back over one's shoulder to Washoe. It's almost like Watergate—"What does she know, and when did she know it?" There is even a videotape whose supposed gaps have come under scrutiny by various factions.

I have dipped into this quagmire sufficiently to have come to the conclusion that there is more to be learned from looking at the quagmire from a distance than by entering it and attempting to determine its shape by peering through the murk. Despite my caution, the quagmire is germane to the fate of the apes in question, and I feel bound to review a couple of its particulars.

The problems of this controversy over ape language are compounded because a number of cognitive scientists have assumed that the debate is settled one way or another and have then gone on to base suppositions on their view of the way in which the debate is settled. For instance, the group charged with reporting on the state of the art in thinking in "Communication as Evidence of Thinking" at the prestigious Dahlem Conference included the following summarizing remarks in its statement: "As a starting point, Terrace argued that we should replace the study of syntax with a more detailed investigation of the meaning of individual signs. This follows from the fact that, whether because of motivational or cognitive deficits, most of the signs made by the chimpanzee in Terrace's study were simply repetitions of signs made shortly before by the animal's trainer." And then later, "Finally, underlying all of these problems is the issue of motivation. Consider, for example, Terrace's point that humans frequently communicate without any apparent attempt to get something. In contrast, to get a lone chimpanzee in a laboratory to say 'red,' you have to give some immediate reward."

The two above points were keystones of the logic of the group's conclusions, and yet both points have been challenged vigorously, not just as they pertain to other ape experiments but as they pertain to Nim. (I have seen enough different apes signing to themselves or to people who don't know sign language or to people who plainly have no rewards to offer to cause me to believe that if Nim acted as Terrace asserts he acted, then he was the anomaly and not the norm.) Terrace was a member of the working group that prepared the report, and consequently it is not surprising that his views on ape sign-language capacity carried such weight, but Terrace's facts are not everybody's facts. It's as though a sixteenth-century astronomical society decided that when, under Vatican pressure, Galileo recanted his belief in a heliocentric solar system, the matter was then settled, and they could get back to business as usual.

The result of this schizophrenic situation is that whenever one encounters a theory or supposition that has the ape language experiments as a take-off point, one has to interpolate backward to determine which reality the theorist is using as his starting point: Terrace's reality, Premack's reality, the Gardners' reality, Patterson's reality, the Rumbaughs' reality, Fouts's reality, and so on. They don't seem to have that much in common.

For the past few years, the reality that has gotten the most attention has been Terrace's reality. He has spent tremendous energy promoting his views, and while those views are less than enthusiastically endorsed by others in the field, he has enjoyed some success in persuading influential outsiders that his explanation of chimp use of sign language is the appropriate one. As noted earlier, Terrace himself succinctly summed up his view a few years back in the *New York Review of Books* when he wrote that a sign-language-using chimp was doing nothing more than "running on with its hands until it gets what it wants."

Terrace did not always hold that view, and this is why he is such a darling of the "rejection front" in this debate. He began working with Nim Chimpsky in 1973, telling people at that time that he was going to do what the Gardners did, but he was going to do it right. When he acquired Nim from the Institute for Primate Studies, the chimp already had a vocabulary of about a dozen words. Terrace, whose previous work had been concerned with the strict behaviorist training of pigeons, at first tried a tough regime of rewards and punishments on Nim. According to a woman connected with the experiment at that time, Nim's vocabulary promptly fell. Terrace quickly abandoned that approach and began to frankly imitate the training methods of Roger Fouts.

During the course of the experiment, Terrace used videotape to monitor the interchanges between ape and human. In his study of Nim's word use, Terrace analyzed about three and a half hours of videotape (taken from about nine hours of videotape that was the basis of a graduate student's dissertation), and according to Terrace, it was this examination that led him to change his mind about what Nim was up to when he was signing. Three and a half hours of videotape does not seem like much of a sample, given that the experiment went on for years, but it should be kept in mind that analyzing videotape is an extremely time-consuming operation. For instance, it took twenty hours for one psychologist to analyze eight minutes of tape. A more serious question would be how representative the three and a half hours of tape were.

Terrace said that before examining the tape, he was convinced he was going to make a major breakthrough in analyzing the syntactic characteristics of Nim's multiple-sign combinations. Indeed his book *Nim* reads as though he never had the slightest doubt about Nim's abilities until he examined the videotapes. Terrace claims that an analysis of the videotapes showed that Nim's statements were most often repetitions of words he had just seen his instructors make. He rarely seemed to take the lead in initiating a conversation. Moreover, Terrace noted that Nim interrupted a great deal and did not seem to understand the interactive nature of conversation. Finally Terrace claims that an analysis of Nim's multi-word statements showed that little additional information was introduced with added length.

So far, so good (although as noted earlier, there are a number of analysts who dispute the validity of Terrace's conclusions about Nim), but in a number of conferences and meetings, Terrace has gone further, claiming that his examination of the data produced by other ape language experiments has convinced him that the same conclusions can be drawn with respect to Washoe, Koko, and all the other language-using apes. And this brings us to a questionable thirty-five seconds of videotape.

Terrace examined a film, *Teaching Sign Language to the Chimpanzee: Washoe*, taken of Washoe during her time in Reno with the Gardners. The Gardners, for their part, have not made any pretense that the film demonstrates Washoe's command of syntax. Washoe was made uneasy by the cameras and crew, and the film was designed to show nothing more than Washoe's vocabulary. Still, Terrace has treated the film as though it were representative of Washoe's use of sign language. Terrace argued in *Science* magazine and elsewhere that the film showed that Washoe's sign combinations were imitations of her teachers' signs. He also examined parts of the film for evidence of the failings demonstrated by Nim.

Out of the thirty-nine minutes of film which showed interactions, Terrace chose to examine thirty-five seconds, ostensibly because that was the longest unedited sequence of film that showed any interaction. Terrace claims that in this brief snippet Washoe interrupted Beatrice Gardner three out of the four times that Dr. Gardner began to make a sign. Ergo: Washoe no more understands the interactive nature of language than did Nim.

Roger Fouts, along with three other psychologists—Chris O'Sullivan, Mark Hannum (who actually performed the analysis), and Katie Schneider—took the trouble to examine the same snippet of film and Terrace's critique. They noted that during that same sequence, Beatrice Gardner interrupted Washoe twice and gave her "the wrong behavioral signals" another time. They then went on to examine the method by which Terrace arrived at his conclusion.

Terrace had based his analysis on the individual frames that showed each sign the most clearly. The four psychologists counter-argued that, given the nature of sign language, it is not possible to judge an interruption the way one would if the interruption occurred in spoken English. Specifically, they noted, "Simultaneous signing is comprehensible by both conversants. The rates of interruption must be determined by such variables as eye contact, hand position, body orientation, signing motion, and content. Isolated frames may be inadequate to capture the interplay of hands, eyes, and body orientation, much less sign continuity."

The group then made a further examination of the points during the thirty-five seconds during which Dr. Gardner and Washoe either held the floor or gave up the floor. These are called "turn signals," and the psychologists' reading of the film produced only three out of seventeen turn signals that were in doubt.

Fouts, Hannum, and another psychologist, Robert Ingersoll, also constructed their own experiment to determine Nim's understanding of conversation, once Terrace had returned the chimp to Oklahoma. They filmed Nim and another chimp named Mac (who had not been encouraged to sign in the two previous years) in interaction with human beings who either knew sign language or did not. What the various factions talked about was entirely up to them—the experimenters were only concerned with the etiquette of holding or giving up the floor. They analyzed the films of the interactions for such variables as eye contact, body orientation, physical contact, signs, human interruptions, and chimpanzee interruptions. "The results of the experiment show that the human beings involved were not as competent as the chimpanzees in the regulatory system of ASL. Nim interrupted his human companions only twice, whereas the humans interrupted Nim a total of seven times. . . ."

Thus something as simple as twenty frames of a film designed to show Washoe's ability to make signs is used as proof of two different realities. Where does that leave us? Carolyn Ristau and Donald Robbins did an extensive survey and interpretation of all the different language experiments, and they had this to say after examining the arguments advanced by various scientists:

> Terrace et al. concluded that their present evidence suggests that ape language learning is severely restricted. He and his colleagues consider that apes can learn many isolated symbols, but state

that there is no unequivocal evidence that apes can master conversational, semantic, and syntactic aspects of language. We have no reason to disagree with Terrace's conclusions. *Realize, however, what this means* [emph. mine]. Methods of data collection and analysis to date do *not* let us determine the limits of the apes' ability, nor do they much help us to understand the meaning inherent in the apes' productions. Concluding that there is no *unequivocal* evidence is an extremely conservative position to take. To be sure, there are problems with some of the methods and interpretations of projects by the Gardners, Fouts, and Patterson. These problems create enough uncertainty so that one is unwilling to take a position supporting some of their claims. On the other hand, there are methodological and interpretive problems inherent in the Nim project—thus, the conclusions drawn from the project must also cause one some misgivings. We do not suggest rejecting all available data, but rather consider what each project has demonstrated in an effort to refine further the data collection techniques and our interpretative abilities.... Apes *may* be more proficient than Terrace intimates; the data do not at all dismiss that alternative.

In sum, one cannot unequivocally say anything either negative or positive about the results of the experiments.

Although I am far more skeptical of Terrace's conclusions than these two observers seem to be—I feel that Terrace transformed the failure of his experiment into a failure of chimpanzees—I do not think that Robbins and Ristau take an unreasonable position. What they stress is that all Terrace has done is to have raised doubts about what Nim was doing when he used signs. He has not *proven* anything about the limitations of a chimpanzee capacity for language. And yet for much of the scientific

community and for much of the informed public, Project
Nim is perceived to be the last word, the proof that apes,
as Martin Gardner put it once, are no smarter than pigs,
bright enough as animals go, but no threat to the temple
of language. And this perception, and the zeal with
which Terrace has promoted it, has given such experiments a bad name in the universities where such research might be undertaken and among the private
foundations and government agencies that formerly sup-
ported the work.

Thus, Terrace's reality has gradually become something of a self-fulfilling prophecy, in that it has had the
effect of cutting off funding for further experiments that
might contradict his version. Looking back on what has
happened, George Kimball remarked, "In a lot of ways
what Herbie did was our own fault. We had data sitting
in drawers in our offices that would contradict his statements about Washoe, but we didn't get it out."

As Kimball's remark indicates, the debate became
personalized to some extent with "Herbie" symbolizing
the opposition in the debate about ape language abilities.
And while some of the critics have murmured about
fraud, the proponents are not above hitting back below
the belt. I introduced Roger Fouts at a talk at the Smithsonian Institution in which he put such emphasis on the
fact that Terrace is a lifelong bachelor that the word took
on a sinister connotation. He then went on to say that
without having raised children, Terrace did not have the
basis in human experience for making judgments about
ape abilities. Thus, while the proponents temporized,
Terrace held the floor as the most passionate champion.

Some of the information that Kimball said was sitting
in desk drawers is now beginning to come out. Two of
the Gardners' graduate students, Thomas E. Van Cant-
fort and James B. Rimpau, have published a thorough,
point-by-point dissection of criticisms advanced by Terrace and *his* graduate students, Michael Seidenberg and
Laura Petito.

There are also some signs of renewed interest in ape language abilities, but the attention has shifted from chimpanzees to other species. At the University of Tennessee at Chattanooga, Dr. H. Lyn Miles has been working with an orangutan named Chantek. Lyn Miles has taught Chantek over one hundred signs in Ameslan, and she has focused her study to explore what critics have described as deficiencies in other language studies. For instance, she has devoted a good deal of time to studying various levels of reference in Chantek's use of sign language. One of the more intriguing things she has done has been to teach Chantek a rudimentary economic system—something Roger dreamed of doing with chimps years ago. For doing such things as cleaning up her room, the orangutan earns tokens which she can spend later in the day on food and special treats of various sorts.

Duane Rumbaugh and Sue Savage-Rumbaugh, who earlier washed their hands of ape language work, are also back in business, only this time they are working with pygmy chimpanzees. Since these rare apes became available for study in captivity a few years ago, they have had a profound effect on the people who have encountered them. They appear more humanlike, and according to observers, they act more human than the other great apes. Sue Savage-Rumbaugh, who was a strident critic of the sign-language experiments, has become a great champion of pygmy chimp language abilities, according to news accounts and reports of scientists.

But perhaps the most telling sign that the times may be changing again is that one of the consultants on this experiment is Herb Terrace. A scientist who visited the experiment told me that when a National Institute of Health official asked Terrace how someone so globally negative on the subject of ape language abilities could consult on such a project, he admitted that Nim's performance might have been the result of a problem in experimental design rather than his lack of capabilities.

Unfortunately, if indeed Terrace has recanted, he has only done so privately. And while Terrace was perhaps its most visible critic, the rehabilitation of ape language research in the eyes of other scientists, funding agencies, and the public is more than just a simple matter of Herb Terrace's saying that he was wrong. At the present moment it is unclear whether it is too late to rescue language studies with apes from the quagmire.

In the meantime, the veterans of the earlier experiments with chimpanzees have found their lives radically affected by the years during which their demoralized advocates allowed Terrace and the other critics to have center stage. The diminished estimation of the language abilities of Nim and other apes during recent years has had effects on all the sign-language-using chimps, as well as indirect effects on the lives of all laboratory chimps in the United States.

In Terrace's reality, the chimpanzee is just another animal, sensitive and intelligent, to be sure, but with none of the abilities that together constitute what we call the human soul: the capacity to construct a world with words, to retrieve and communicate experiences from the past, to discuss the nature of life and death. In Terrace's neo-Cartesian world, the ethical problem that would be posed by language-using animals does not exist; without language, chimpanzees are only entitled to such rights as we might confer on them out of our humanity, and not such rights as they might enjoy as creatures who shared language and reasoning skills with humanity. And the events of the past few years suggest that, stripped of the protective magic of language, the only protection chimps enjoy is that afforded by their high price tag and relative scarcity.

Chimp Bites Man

CHAPTER SIX

Winding Down

WHILE the critics were gearing up, many of the experiments were beginning to wind down. But in the mid-1970s there was a curious, contradictory confluence of forces at work on the experiments. While funding was beginning to dry up, undergraduates still flocked to the various projects.

By this time, the sign-language experiments were sufficiently well known that undergraduates began to tailor their studies with an eye to eventually taking part in the work. This new generation did not come out of laboratory disciplines as so many earlier behavioral scientists had. Many of them came to the work with the idea that chimps were cohabitants of the planet rather than objects of study. Thus, while the circumstances of chimps at the institute were certainly better than the circumstances of chimps in medical experimentation, they were still something of a shock to the new graduate students eager to begin talking with man's closest relative. Padlocked collars, nylon dog leads, pellet guns, cattle prods, and the other accoutrements of the uneasy authority humanity exercised over chimps somewhat shocked students who expected to see people and chimps walking hand in hand into the sunset. In recent years, more than one veteran of the institute has told me that I was partly to blame for this culture shock by making the institute seem more idyllic than it was. However, others agree with me that in the early 1970s life was more pleasant at the institute than it had become by the mid-1970s.

One of the new generation was a young woman named Janis Carter. A plump, independent, and legendarily stubborn woman, Janis Carter grew up leading the peripatetic life of an Air Force brat. She came to the University of Oklahoma specifically to work on sign-language experimentation. She later told me that her interest was first piqued by my book *Apes, Men, and Language,* which she read as part of her psychology studies at the University of Tennessee.

Janis was always idealistic, and she reacted strongly to what she felt were unnecessarily harsh constraints used on the chimps. She had a falling out with William Lemmon, and although she was only in Oklahoma a little more than a year, it was a year marked by turmoil, according to Janis and to those who knew her then. She never really got into sign-language work, although she took sign-language lessons, as did all the graduate students who would be working with those chimps that had been taught Ameslan. After a few months, Janis got a job helping to take care of Lucy and Marianne (a chimp the Temerlins had acquired the previous year as a companion for Lucy). This got her away from the institute and away from direct confrontations with Lemmon.

Janis happened to arrive at a moment when the Temerlins were beginning to wonder about Lucy's future. Perhaps because she was part of a household rather than a chimp colony, the question of what to do with the full-grown chimp was more immediate and pressing than it would have been at the institute. Lucy was eleven years old in 1975, and the Temerlins' house and furnishings offered about the same resistance to Lucy that a house of balsa wood might offer to an exuberant human adolescent. Moreover, the Temerlins could envision a day in the future when their tenuous dominance over Lucy might break down utterly. What could they do if one day Lucy simply refused to obey them? And besides, the Temerlins wanted to live a normal life again. Like so many others who dealt with chimps on a day to day basis, they found themselves worn out by the climate of demands that follows from the mere fact of having a chimpanzee around the house.

There was also the question of deteriorating relations between Lemmon and the Temerlins. According to his book *Lucy, Growing Up Human*, Maury Temerlin returned from a trip to Esalen determined to take control of his life. This entailed severing relations with a certain figure who had dominated him for so long. The break also eliminated the possibility of sending Lucy to the Institute for Primate Studies. But neither did the Temerlins wish to consign Lucy to life in a zoo or game park.

Jane Temerlin says that they first began to think about what to do with Lucy in about 1974, when active sign-language work with Lucy began to decline. Over the next two years they spoke with Jane Goodall, Sue Savage-Rumbaugh, and a number of other people in primate work.

Although Jane Temerlin does not remember precisely, she says that in late 1976 or early 1977 she and her husband heard about Stella Brewer's work in rehabilitating chimps in the wild. They heard about Brewer from William McGrew, a primatologist who had been in Norman but who was then at the University of Edinburgh. "Once we heard that it might be possible to give Lucy a life in the wild," says Jane Temerlin, "we began to think seriously about the prospect." The reaction around the university was "guarded at best," she says. "People did not come out and say the idea was nutty, but they let us know that they thought it was nearly impossible."

Still, the Temerlins had to do something. Lucy was

not only full grown but, as Jane puts it, "reproductively needy" (meaning that she developed explicit crushes on people). If they did not come to some decision soon, they feared she would be forever denied the possibility of a normal life with other chimps.

At this time, Stella Brewer had about six chimpanzees that she and her associates were attempting to rehabilitate. She had grown up in Africa, but rehabilitating chimps requires more than a knowledge of the bush. Stella Brewer is the daughter of Eddie Brewer, a white ex-colonial who is Director of Wildlife in The Gambia. The Gambia is a tiny country in West Africa that consists of little more than the banks of the river Gambia. The park system Eddie Brewer presides over is made up of a small reserve outside Banjul, the capital, and a couple of islands located 136 miles upstream from the capital. Brewer and his daughter began trying to rehabilitate chimpanzees to the wild, at first in Niokolo Koba National Park in Senegal, and then later in the Baboon Islands in The Gambia.

When first approached, Stella Brewer was reluctant to take Lucy on, and with good reason. Lucy was fully grown and had no previous experience with the wild. There were no precedents for rehabilitating a fully grown chimpanzee, and Lucy certainly was not a prime candidate for life in the wild by any standard. She had been born and raised in the United States, and in pampered upper-middle-class circumstances. Lucy slept on a mattress, sipped soda, developed schoolgirl crushes, and would sit in the living room during the afternoon and leaf through magazines. She was a regular little Private Benjamin.

Even worse, she had no experience with other chimpanzees except for her short exposure to Marianne. Finally, Stella Brewer did not have the prior relationship with Lucy necessary to give her dominance over the chimp.

The communications between the Brewers and the

Temerlins occurred not long after Janis Carter had begun working with Lucy. "Janis had developed a good relationship with Lucy," says Jane Temerlin, "which was unusual because she had not been with Lucy for long and because Lucy was full grown. She shared our concern about Lucy—we would have long talks—and when we asked her whether she would consider the possibility of going with Lucy to Africa, she jumped at the chance."

The offer to have someone accompany Lucy and ease the transition ultimately caused Stella Brewer to change her mind. For the Temerlins, who could see no attractive alternative destiny for Lucy at home, it seemed like a worthwhile gamble. Whatever happened, at least Lucy would have a chance to lead the life nature had crafted her to lead.

Maury, Jane, Janis, Lucy, and Marianne left for Africa in September 1977. Roger Fouts had come by to say good-bye to Lucy and to accompany the group to the airport, but a normal conversation was impossible given what Jane describes as a chaotic scene (Roger had enjoyed a more tranquil farewell the previous night).

Lucy and Marianne were to ride in crates, something Lucy had never done before; efforts to tranquilize the chimps with an oral dose of ketamine backfired as Lucy became more and more indignant. Finally they administered a shot, the two chimps quieted down, and the group was able to set off.

The trip itself was relatively uneventful, except for the emotions it inspired in the Temerlins, who, although they had made the decision themselves, did not find letting go easy. Still, it was in retrospect a somewhat haphazard expedition. The idea that Lucy, the fastidious, toilet-trained chimpanzee princess, could make it in the wild stretched the odds to the limit. And despite Janis's willingness to accompany Lucy and despite her relationship with the chimp, there was little in her background to suggest that Janis was prepared for the rigors she would face. She did not like camping even in the United States!

And then there was the unknown of Stella Brewer's operation: how successful was her work, and what kind of hardships would Lucy have to endure? On the face of it, the concept of turning Lucy into a wild chimp seemed quixotic at best.

And indeed, the first few months of the experience seemed to bear out all those who felt that the plan was ill conceived. The Temerlins returned after about a week, but Janis says that she could see almost from the moment she arrived that there was no possibility that she would return to the United States in a few weeks, as planned. For one thing, according to Janis, the Brewers were totally unprepared for their arrival. They had made no provision for Lucy and Marianne, and so, at Abuko Reserve (Lucy's first home in Africa), the two chimps were transferred to steel cages that were far more primitive than anything in use at the Institute for Primate Studies. Lucy went into a decline from the moment she arrived and within weeks was an emaciated, hairless wreck—the kind of picture that might show up as the alarmist photo on the cover of a radical animal rights publication. Because it was feared that once she left her cage, no one would be able to get her back into it, the cage could not be properly cleaned, and her circumstances rapidly degenerated into utter squalor.

Marianne fared a little better. She had not led a life so privileged as Lucy's, and the transition, while traumatic, was still less stressful than it was for Lucy.

Nor did Janis make any headway in her efforts to help Lucy to learn the ways of a wild chimp. "I would give her netto [a sweet, edible seed pod], and she would throw it away," Janis recalled later on. She tried everything to teach Lucy wild behavior. She would sign to her, talk to her, and in general try to bring the wilds to her. But given the circumstances, it is little wonder that these early lessons bore little fruit. Abuko Reserve is right on the outskirts of Banjul, well served by roads and frequently visited by tourists and locals. The complex where Lucy and Marianne were kept was a zoolike series of cages. While there remained the promise that Lucy might eventually move to the Baboon Islands or to a park in Senegal, the immediate reality was that though Lucy was in Africa, she was in a zoo, and not a zoo that compared favorably with zoos in the United States.

To all appearances, the effort was a dismal failure, and Janis says that after about a year the Temerlins wrote her to that effect and urged her to come home. Feeling the financial burden, they also greatly reduced her support. There was reason to believe that Janis Carter would soon return to the United States. But she didn't.

CHAPTER SEVEN

In Re Sequoyah

IF, AS THE decade waned, things were not going well in Africa for Lucy, the situation was not all that much brighter in Oklahoma or, for that matter, at the other language experiments. The changed times were not exclusively a product of Herb Terrace and the other critics. In fact, a type of polarization occurred in both the pro and con camps. It was not a matter of Terrace's positing a separate reality from everybody else but rather a question of everybody's defensively retreating into the version of reality they believed to be reality.

The vast chasm that separated the realities of those ostensibly within the same camp became clear as opinion crystallized around a couple of events. It was these events that precipitated the unraveling that ultimately had such a devastating effect on the chimp colony. Ironically the first of these events should have been a cause for celebration; to compound the irony, a couple of Washoe's actions contributed to the decline of the Institute for Primate Studies in equal measure with the change of mood abetted by the more vituperative critics.

At the outset of the ape language experiments, there appeared to be a good deal of cross-fertilization among the different disciplines concerned with the subject matter, and a good deal of cooperative effort among the various experimenters. The work was young, and the market, so to speak, was expanding. Graduate students were happy just to be a part of the work and perhaps were in some awe of the pioneers of the field. However, from roughly 1976 onward, the "market," in the sense of financial and academic support for the work, began to contract. Moreover, the veteran graduate students had become familiar enough with the experiments to develop their own ideas about how the work ought to be pursued. And, perhaps most subtly, some of the scientists became so deeply involved in their work that the distinction between personality and science began to blur. And so, while in the past various experimenters had presented a united front to the world, factions and violent disputes began to emerge for the first time.

During my first few visits to Oklahoma, I witnessed very little divisiveness, although I knew that Roger Fouts's relationship with Lemmon was strained. By 1979, those strains had produced a kind of paranoia in Roger, and during a visit that year, the melodramatic nature of that dispute eclipsed another dispute to which I should have paid more attention, and which, as much as anything else, brought Roger to the point where it seemed he had to choose between his commitment to science and his relationship with Washoe.

The reason I visited Oklahoma in 1979 had to do with an event that Roger had been hoping for since he first brought Washoe to Oklahoma. On January 8, 1979, Washoe gave birth to a baby, a male chimpanzee who was given the name Sequoyah, after the superlatively gifted Native American who invented the Cherokee alphabet. It had been Roger's dream that Washoe would bear an infant, and that Roger might study the transmission of sign language across chimpanzee generations. Earlier Washoe had given birth to another infant, but this baby, born with congenital deformities, died just a few days after birth when it fell off a shelf on which Washoe had put it.

The latest happy event stirred the imagination with the prospect of a cornucopia of scientific riches. Would the infant pick up signs at all? Would Washoe actively instruct the baby, or would it imitate the gestures that were so much a part of the mother's life? How would it understand the gestures: as symbols, or as mere triggers for rewards? And so on.

The event was a godsend to Roger in ways totally separate from its scientific interest. The prospect of this intergenerational experiment got Roger a $300,000 grant from the National Science Foundation at a time when the pool of funding for language work with apes was rapidly drying up. But more important, Roger for the first time got a major grant without having Lemmon as a coprincipal investigator. With his $300,000, Roger had a measure of independence from Lemmon, and if this did not improve relations with Lemmon, it did give Roger a temporary measure of confidence. "I'm learning to stand up to daddy," he would joke to colleagues, although by some accounts he still got the shakes before meetings with his former boss.

It was because of this grant that Roger started taking Washoe out again. For some time before the grant, Roger had stopped his walks with Washoe because of the potential dangers. However, if he was to work with Washoe and her infant in a small cage, he had first to reestablish his rapport with Washoe, and this meant taking her out again. Reportedly Roger was at first anxious about reinaugurating these walks after so many months, but he relaxed as he discovered that the hiatus had not undermined his authority.

* * *

WHEN I went to visit Roger in 1979, Washoe had a baby, but it was not Sequoyah. Sequoyah, Washoe's natural infant, was by then dead. The baby I saw with Washoe was a year-old chimp named Loulis, who had come from the Emory-Yerkes Institute outside Atlanta. Determining what had happened to Sequoyah became the center of an intense debate that brought a number of simmering passions to the surface and that ultimately involved interpretations of forensic evidence that might have seemed more appropriate in a murder trial.

In 1979 I was content to accept Roger's version of Sequoyah's death. There was no hint of controversy in press accounts of the event, and though I knew that the event had caused an open breach between Roger and Lemmon, their hostility was old news, and I tended to discount the latest installment of their bickering.

But I shouldn't have. Maternal behavior in chimps is something that Lemmon knows a good deal about. While he is something of a peripheral figure to the field of maternal behavior in the scientific sense, his facility at the time had one of the best breeding records in the United States. Later, when I spoke to Lemmon to try to sort out what actually happened in 1979, a lot of what he said about chimp sexuality and maternal behavior was confirmed by others who are accepted as experts in the field.

I should mention here that in our infrequent meetings I found Lemmon somewhat strange. He is a huge, bald man, and he speaks with an orotund formality in one-to-one encounters. In an odd reversal of what one might expect, he is reputedly very natural in speaking before groups.

I should also mention that after my initial exposure, I became increasingly less enchanted with the life that chimps led at the institute. I began to see some of the discomfiting realities of the lives of the chimps. True, the complex of cages did interconnect, which allowed the keepers to isolate chimps or let them get together in groups, but there is no escaping the dreariness of the concrete and steel structure, particularly since a chronic shortage of funds left the institute without the manpower to keep the area clean. I will go into the problems of the institute a little later, but it is worth noting that disenchantment with the institute was fairly general by the late 1970s, and this made Roger's disagreements with Lemmon seem like something more than a mere personal feud. Noted anthropologist Jane Lancaster, who is affiliated with the University of Oklahoma, refused to work at the institute, although she had done extensive work with primates. "It was sort of like saying, 'I love humans; I think I'll go to the state penitentiary and learn about humans,'" she said in explaining her reluctance.

Given my own reservations about Lemmon and the institute, I was, as I've said, willing to believe Roger's version of events (although I always discounted some of his more extravagant accusations and theories) during our conversations. Here follows an account of Washoe's travails which I recounted in the course of an article I wrote in 1979:

> ...recent events in Washoe's life have been downright melodramatic. For the past three years Fouts had been hoping that Washoe would raise a child. She gave birth twice and lost both babies, the first because of congenital deformities and the second [this was Sequoyah], after three months, to pneumonia.
>
> In both cases, the death was a severe blow to Washoe. She could see that her first baby was dying and, touchingly, handed it to Fouts in hopes that he could save it. When it was discovered that the second baby had a severe bronchial infection, Fouts had to take the infant away for intensive medical care. It died soon afterward, and he had to break the news to Washoe.

The next day he visited her quarters. Immediately she rushed up to him and signed, "Where's baby?" inflecting the question with her eyes as is often done in Ameslan. The sign for "baby" is made by forming the hand in cradle configuration in front of one's body. When Fouts told her the baby was dead, Washoe slumped, dropped her hands into her lap, and stared off into a corner. For the next two days, Washoe rushed up to Fouts whenever she saw him and asked each time, "Where's baby?" He had to tell her that her baby was dead, and again Washoe sat, staring.

The account was accurate as far as it went, but it leaves the impression that Washoe was nothing less than an exemplary, caring mother. That is not the impression of many other observers, including a number who were involved in monitoring Washoe during those critical days. The controversy focuses on how Sequoyah developed that "severe bronchial infection."

For a time, Roger was convinced that either someone had put something in the chimps' food, or that the heater in the converted pig barn where Washoe and Sequoyah were sequestered had been maliciously turned off. (In fact, the barn was notoriously cold.) He hinted that the culprit was either Lemmon or someone in his camp. As is evident from the description of events cited above, I did not put much stock in those theories even at the time. On the other hand, I was not aware of, nor did Roger mention, an alternative explanation being considered by a good number of people involved with the experiment: that Sequoyah died as a result of the cumulative insults of Washoe's neglect and abuse of her infant.

As noted earlier, Washoe was distrusted by a number of the men and women working at the institute. Tales of her aggression against people were legend. For instance, she had bitten David Rowe, a graduate student, on the cheek. The movement had begun as an openmouthed kiss. Aggression camouflaged as affection summed up Washoe for many of those at the institute, and her history in this regard had much to do with the credibility of the alternative explanation of the death of Sequoyah. Even Roger was aware of Washoe's unpredictability, although he ascribed it to a characteristic shared, in his view, by all female chimps. This was what he called "Treacherous Attack." While male chimps work themselves up to aggressive actions and give human beings ample notice of their mounting displeasure, Roger claims that female chimps often use guile to lure the object of their anger into a false sense of security before attacking. Still, there were a number of other female chimps at the institute, and none aroused negative feelings to the degree that Washoe did.

She was perceived by many on the staff as a likely candidate to star in a chimp *Mommie Dearest*. She even turned out to be a jealous lover. Roger noted this when he watched a triangle emerge involving Washoe, Sequoyah's father, and another chimp named Vanessa. The father was none other than Ally. He had been transferred from the main chimp colony into a cage that could be interconnected with Washoe's. Once Washoe became pregnant, she ceased to give off signals that she wanted to mate. On the other hand, Roger discovered that Washoe did not want Ally to mate with anyone else. Vanessa was housed in a cage adjoining, though not interconnecting with, Ally's. Vanessa went into estrus, and Ally abandoned Washoe and began to mate with Vanessa through the wire mesh. This threw Washoe into a rage. She could not get at Vanessa, but she could get at Ally. Roger claims that on one occasion when she caught them mating, she bit Ally on the rear and knocked him almost across the cage. From this point on, Ally, an inveterate philanderer, arranged his assignations for moments when Washoe was distracted.

There is a good deal of evidence that maternal behavior in chimps is not entirely automatic but, rather, is "culturally integrated," to use Lemmon's term. This means that chimps learn to be mothers in part from observing their own and other chimp mothers during their early years. Washoe, of course, was raised primarily apart from her species, and by humans, and Lemmon and others at the institute doubted that she had acquired the necessary skills, even if she had the interest, for motherhood.

Uncertainties about her abilities as a mother were exacerbated by the structure of the experiment. Because Roger was interested in determining whether Sequoyah would acquire sign language from Washoe, he decided to limit the signing that humans could do in their presence, and also the amount of time that people could spend with them in general. If Sequoyah learned to make signs, Roger did not want to have to answer charges that he had acquired them from human beings rather than from Washoe. Monitoring was done by closed-circuit video cameras trained on the cage from different angles.

While the setup had a superficial appeal from the point of view of controls, it contained what in retrospect could be described as fatal flaws. Roger either failed to anticipate or ignored Washoe's perspective on what was going on. It is important to keep in mind that Washoe had spent the past decade experiencing a gradual decline in her status. She had spent her youth in an "enriched environment" with the constant attention of humans. Recall that when she first came to Oklahoma, she reportedly had been appalled by the sight of other chimps, terming them "black bugs." The next several years saw the amount of attention she received and her standard of living show a steady decline. She had been somewhat spoiled during her youth, and by all accounts she bitterly resented her eclipse. Deprived of her entourage like some dispossessed princess, she found herself among immigrants not nearly so eloquent as she.

Keeping this in mind, one can imagine how Washoe

felt when people began to refuse to sign back to her when she "talked" to them and to spend even less time with her than before. It created ludicrous situations. Because Roger felt sorry for her, he would sometimes furtively sign to her when Sequoyah was asleep, or when the baby was distracted by other things.

Washoe surely noticed that her life was different, and perhaps she also noticed that things had begun to change with the birth of Sequoyah. She certainly was aware that people instantly came running whenever Sequoyah screamed. The humans spent most of their time observing from concealment, and it did not take Washoe long to figure out where they were.

Chris O'Sullivan, who was then a graduate student, was one of the people who observed and worked with Washoe during this time. By her account, no one anticipated this fatal flaw in the design of the experiment, although she notes that once the experiment was in progress, George Kimball realized that its structure was conditioning Washoe to abuse Sequoyah. "If Washoe was manipulative," O'Sullivan says, "it was our fault, not hers." Lemmon is less charitable. "I saw Washoe use her infant to manipulate in ways horrible to contemplate," he says. "In effect she was saying, 'Give me some fruit, or I will put this infant under the faucet.'"

No one has said that Washoe unambiguously hated Sequoyah. I have no reason to believe that Washoe was not profoundly depressed by the infant's death. Rather, it seems that some crucial aspects of mothering were absent, and in the lapses of her maternal feelings, other more selfish feelings would intrude. Lemmon claims that her behavior with her first infant, who fell and cracked its skull, should have been a clue. As a rule, chimp mothers never put down their newborns, and the fact that Washoe put down her first baby should have rung some alarm bells. Neither did Washoe like nursing, and she reacted adversely to Sequoyah's attempts to do so. For a time, Sequoyah was fed on expressed human mother's milk. In fact, Roger asked the female assistants to pretend to breast-feed the baby chimp and then surreptitiously substitute the expressed milk. More than one balked at the idea.

On March 6, 1979, when he was about eight weeks old, Sequoyah died. The diagnosed cause of death was acute respiratory disease, pneumonia; however, the question of how Sequoyah developed that disease ultimately caused the institute to break up into acrimonious camps. Sequoyah died two days after having been found with a toothbrush jammed down his throat.

On the Saturday night before Sequoyah died, Chris O'Sullivan, who, along with an undergraduate, was working the eight P.M. to midnight shift, found a note in the daily log warning people not to give Washoe her toothbrush. Washoe ordinarily used the toothbrush to brush her teeth. Chris did let Washoe brush her teeth but then took the toothbrush back from Washoe and put it away.

On Sunday morning, two project assistants showed up for the eight A.M. to noon shift. According to various accounts, when they arrived, Washoe rushed up to the wire mesh, very upset, and held up Sequoyah, who was seen to have the toothbrush jammed down his throat.

According to Roger Fouts, Roger Mellgren, and a few others, Washoe had been trying to aspirate Sequoyah, who, under the effects of pneumonia, was having difficulty breathing. Examinations revealed that Sequoyah had severe lacerations in his throat, which indicates that the toothbrush was inserted with something other than delicacy. According to M.L. Allen, Diana Davis, Chris O'Sullivan, Lemmon, and a number of others, who were around the institute at the time of the accident, Washoe fatally abused her infant—possibly under the guise of trying to help it. While Roger insists that Sequoyah had pneumonia prior to Washoe's action, the other camp notes that the acute nonviral pneumonia can be brought on by the sort of injuries inflicted by the toothbrush.

Moreover, the posted warning note indicates that this wasnot the first time Washoe had used the toothbrush in an abusive manner.

In a paper delivered at a meeting of the American Society of Primatologists, M.L. Allen noted that "Washoe displayed very low rates of active cradling of her infant Sequoyah, and subsequently fatally abused him."

The argument about what happened developed over a period of months, and in the way of most arguments, it got nastier as it went on. Lemmon said in effect, "I told you so," while Roger hinted broadly that someone had nefariously poisoned Sequoyah or had turned down the heat, which brought on his pneumonia. Diana Davis had been one of Roger's favored graduate students —in fact she had entered enthusiastically into the breastfeeding project. When, a year later, she wrote a paper that questioned Washoe's suitability as a mother, Roger blew up. He accused Diana of calling Washoe a "bad mother." Later he told people that Diana had wanted to mother the infant herself.

Roger had a history of taking criticism of Washoe personally. Long before the dispute over Sequoyah broke out, Roger had reacted to criticisms of the sign-language experiments as though they were an attack on Washoe.

Also, even before Sequoyah died, there had been strains between various people, most of which were hidden behind the increasingly tattered mask of solidarity presented by those at the institute. Today, however, talk to people, and you will hear statements like "I have yet to hear one person [at the institute] say a good word about another person." Chris O'Sullivan says, "Chimp people are the most argumentative group of people of anyone on earth." She adds that they tend to turn scientific arguments into ad hominem attacks.

Despite the now open doubts about Washoe's capacities as a mother, Roger quickly moved to find another infant to replace Sequoyah. He located a ten-month-old chimp at Emory-Yerkes, who was taken from his mother and brought to Oklahoma on March 20, 1979. Diana Davis, who had not yet broken openly with Roger, was one of the people who drove down to Georgia to get the chimp. This exacerbated the disagreements then current, because some of the assistants had doubts about the ethics of taking the infant from its natural mother and delivering it to the questionable affections of Washoe. In fact, prior to the death of Sequoyah, Roger had held forth several times on the evils of separating a baby chimp from its mother.

This infant, named Loulis, was the chimp I saw with Washoe when I visited the institute. According to Roger, Washoe continually asked Roger where her baby was after the infant died. Thus, when he told her that he had a baby for her, Washoe was excited. However, when little Loulis was brought in, she could instantly see that this was not her baby, and she would have nothing to do with Loulis. Loulis, for his part, could see that Washoe was not his mother and didn't want to have anything to do with her.

According to Roger, two days later, Washoe awoke and apparently decided that she wanted the baby in her arms. She stood up and signed, "Come hug," as dramatically as she could. Roger said that Loulis, who at first had failed to understand what Washoe meant by the gesture, jumped into her arms. Loulis is still with Washoe today, seven years later, which Roger feels supports his contention that Washoe really is a good mother.

That Loulis and Washoe enjoyed and continue to enjoy a good relationship may in fact indicate that Washoe is a good mother. Or it may indicate that Loulis was old enough that Washoe did not have to do the things, such as breast-feeding and continually holding the infant, that she did not enjoy doing with Sequoyah.

Loulis has reportedly acquired a good number of signs, although it is open to question who Loulis acquired them from. (More recently Roger and his colleagues used Loulis in a chimp-to-chimp communication study, that was monitored by remote videotape. With no humans present, the chimp group did continue to sign to each other, according to Roger.)

The strains of these births and deaths and arguments caused Roger to more actively consider doing something he had talked about for years—moving the chimps from Oklahoma to some other, more peaceful and more truly wild place. When I visited the Institute for Primate Studies in 1979, Robert Towne, the producer, was also there. At that time, Towne was becoming involved in a movie called *Greystoke* (based on the original Tarzan story), and he and Roger spoke about using Roger's chimps in the movie in return for a facility that would provide for the needs of both scientists and chimps. Roger spoke about other possibilities as well: moving the chimps to Africa or to an island, or joining forces with Penny Patterson or with someone else.

Nor was Roger the only experimenter who wanted to go away with the chimps to some remote, untrammeled place. Penny Patterson actively looked for a safe harbor for herself and Koko before she settled down with Koko and Michael on a farm just a few miles from the Stanford campus, where she had raised the two gorillas.

I can well understand the urge to get away. Even without the stresses of the dispute over Washoe's maternal behavior, the ongoing pressures to defend the work in the face of the repercussions of Terrace's and Thomas Sebeok's energetic attacks, coupled with the fishbowl existence this work becomes once you have opened the gates to publicity, are enough to make anyone dream of a less confusing life.

Long before the tempest over Sequoyah, various people at the institute began to wonder what was going to happen to the chimps. Ally, Booee, and Bruno were fully grown, and purportedly Lemmon was the only person who could handle all of them (although George Kimball still took Ally out periodically). If working with a four-year-old male is like handling a hyperactive NFL line-backer, a ten-year-old male is King Kong. It was simply out of the question for anyone at the institute besides Lemmon to take the risk of going into the cage with the adult males. (I should note here that in other experiments there are cases of people who have established long-term relationships with chimps and gorillas that permit them to work with them into adulthood.)

The adult male chimps could not help growing up, but with each step toward maturity, they also lessened their grip on the affections of those around them. One consequence of this was that their lives became increasingly boring and lonely. Indeed, what was going to become of them?

CHAPTER EIGHT

Chimp
Bites Man

A LITTLE more than a year after the death of Sequoyah, disaster struck again. This time Washoe's victim was a person—no less a person than the esteemed neuroscientist Karl Pribram. The disaster had not so much to do with the amount of damage Washoe inflicted on Pribram as with Pribram's response. Washoe had bitten people before (one recalls the toothed kiss she administered to David Rowe's cheek), but this bite brought into focus a debate over the relationship between the University of Oklahoma and the Institute for Primate Studies. Washoe's action set in motion a chain of events that led to the dispersal of her chimp cohorts to medical labs and zoos around the country.

There is an irony here, because at the time Washoe bit Pribram, she was not physically at the Institute for Primate Studies but at South Base. Not long after the death of Sequoyah, Roger had moved Washoe, Loulis, and Ally to South Base, a former military base owned by the university. The move was precipitated by Roger's desire to get himself and his work out of Lemmon's purview, and it was made possible by the NSF grant which had given him a measure of independence.

Relations between the two men had grown worse from year to year. Lemmon was wont to torture Roger by threatening to sell Washoe. (As we shall see, this was particularly effective because there was some ambiguity about who actually owned Washoe. It was said that Lemmon once even jokingly informed Roger that he had sold Roger.) Roger knew that South Base was at best a temporary refuge and began actively looking for a place to take his brood.

While it had established a greater physical distance between Roger and Lemmon, one casualty of the move to South Base was Ally's few moments of freedom. George Kimball said that at the institute they could seal off the driveway to keep passersby away from Ally, but that at South Base there was no way to ensure against accidental meetings of chimps and people. A few times, George took a chance and drove Ally to an isolated water tower and let him clamber around, but the uncertainties and dangers eventually convinced him that it was better not to take such risks. Thus 1979 was the last time Ally has been outside a cage, unrestrained and unsedated.

Washoe's misdeed at South Base was not particularly dramatic. In April 1980, Karl Pribram was visiting the institute and stopped at Washoe's cage at a moment when an assistant, Jill Camp, was feeding her through the wires. Pribram, who had decades of experience with primates, reportedly said, "Can I help?" When he reached through the wires with some food, Washoe grabbed one of his fingers in her teeth.

Here again there is dispute about what the action meant. Roger asserts that Washoe merely held Pribram's finger in her teeth. According to this theory, Pribram hurt himself by pulling back in alarm and scraping his finger against the sharp wire cage. Pribram alleges that

Washoe bit with intent to hurt, and further, that she has a history of biting. The wound did become infected, and eventually part of the finger had to be amputated.

At some point, the idea occurred to Pribram to sue Washoe, or at least to sue those who could be held liable for her actions, but before this happened, there was to be more melodrama at the Institute for Primate Studies. The Central Washington University in Ellensburg, Washington, offered Roger a post as well as a facility for his chimps. Roger decided to resign from the University of Oklahoma (where he had tenure), and his resignation was announced on July 21, 1980. However, there was a minor snag in that the facility in Washington was not yet quite ready to receive Washoe, Loulis, and a chimp called Moja, who'd been taught Ameslan during the Gardners' second experiment and then given to Roger.

For Roger, who by now had convinced himself that Lemmon would stop at nothing to make his life miserable, the delay was intolerable. In fact, there was a custody battle over who actually owned Washoe, which was brought to a head by Roger's decision to leave. Lemmon claimed that he had taken ownership of Washoe when he agreed to accept her from Beatrice Gardner. Roger claimed that Washoe was actually owned by the Air Force, who had given the chimp to Beatrice Gardner, who had then given Washoe to Roger. There was enough ambiguity for Roger to convince himself that Lemmon might kidnap or otherwise prevent him from taking Washoe with him to Ellensburg. Roger decided to get out of Oklahoma whether or not the Ellensburg facility was ready.

Roger arranged for a truck with cages suitable for chimps to come to Norman from Gentle Jungle in Riverside, California. Gentle Jungle is a commercial animal-training facility. When the truck left Norman "in the dead of night" (as one observer noted) on August 25, it contained the chimps along with Roger and Ken DeCroo, from Gentle Jungle. Roger departed on such short notice that two students who had intended to come along were left behind. Also left behind was Roger's wife, Debbi, who tidied up matters in Oklahoma and then went to Ellensburg to prepare for Roger and the chimps' arrival. Roger and the other refugees from Norman spent a little more than a month at Gentle Jungle before heading north to Ellensburg. (It is interesting to note that animal activists have since succeeded in having Gentle Jungle closed down for its inhumane treatment of the animals housed there.)

Back in Oklahoma, Washoe left a legacy in the form of a lawsuit. Pribram claimed that the injury had damaged his ability to pursue his career as a neurosurgeon and sued Roger Fouts, the University of Oklahoma, and William Lemmon as the maker of the cages (when Lemmon agreed to let Fouts move to South Base, he insisted on building and selling to Roger the cages in which the chimps would be kept). Fouts pointed out that Pribram had not practiced neurosurgery in thirty years. Animal rights groups pointed out that the only surgery Pribram had been practicing had been vivisection of apes, and that there was some justice in Washoe's revenge. (In the face of all this bad publicity, Pribam decided to drop his suits.) And during all of this, university officials began to wonder about other liability suits that might follow from the eleven fingers and one thumb that purportedly had also been lost as a result of chimp bites during the history of the institute. For this and other reasons the university pressed with new urgency a study it had commissioned of its relationship with the institute.

Lemmon was to discover that however nettlesome he may have felt Fouts to be, his presence had given the Institute for Primate Studies a cachet that Lemmon by himself could not. There were not that many PhDs produced by the institute in the best of times, and without Fouts there would be a lot fewer. Lemmon simply did not have the reputation to attract graduate students, nor did he have the ongoing research program to attract the massive funding that would be needed to improve the animal housing and care at the institute.

I talked with a number of people familiar with the institute during the period after Fouts had left. While there was a feeling that Lemmon did the best with what he had, still the institute presented the university with a host of liabilities and with very little in the way of benefits. There was the possibility that because the institute did not meet minimal federal standards for cleanliness, the university might lose other federal money for other programs at the university and its medical school. The institute was a private facility, which meant that the university had no control over its policies. Thus, the university had no legal rights at the institute, but a passel of unwanted potential embarrassments.

The deliberations over the institute's future occurred in the midst of a deepening recession and at a time when the full brunt of Reaganomics was affecting the sciences. Federal money, which is the lifeblood of research, was drying up like a puddle in the Mohave in July, and this fact influenced the debate about the future of the institute. Lemmon jokingly said later, "It was a black day for chimpanzees when Bonzo bit Ronald Reagan."

Ultimately the committee of outside consultants appointed to study the university's relationship to the institute reported that the institute needed a great deal of money put into it if it was to be able to meet federal standards or to ensure the safety of its staff. In the face of the report, the suit by Pribram, and the void in primate studies created by Fouts's departure, the university decided to sever all ties with the institute.

When I spoke to Lemmon in April 1982, two months before the university was officially to terminate its support of the institute, he was alternately philosophical and bitter. He was feisty on the subject of government money, saying that "any place in which a government contract comes first is a bad place for a chimp." He said proudly that the institute was one of only three labs in the country not under "government domination." The bitterness had to do with the nature of Roger's departure. "It came down to the fact that I couldn't control Roger, and after ten years of feeding and caring for Washoe, I am bitter," he said.

I must admit that given the extremely negative things Lemmon had to say about Washoe as a mother and as a personality, I would have thought that he would have been delighted to see the last of her. But such is the nature of the world of primate studies that just as you get used to thinking about a chimp as a personality, as almost human, the context shifts, and it becomes property.

Actually the biting incident brought into collision three distinct attitudes toward Washoe. There was Pribram, for whom Washoe was a "wild and dangerous animal" not responsible for her actions, and suitable for research to understand human problems. There was Roger, for whom Washoe was a soul-mate to be rescued from the clutches of Lemmon and the institute. And there was Lemmon, who could see Washoe as an individual and who is protective of chimp rights, but for whom ultimately chimps are a form of property. Finally, what we don't know are Washoe's feelings about herself and her place in the universe.

Chimps, particularly sign-language-using chimps, really do pose a conundrum. To treat Washoe's bite as the act of a dumb beast might make a certain amount of sense legally, but it would not ring true to anyone who had spent time with her. Alternatively it would be equally absurd to take the position that because she knew language, she, and not her keepers, was responsible for her actions. One envisions Washoe on the witness stand, lamenting in sign language the increasing loss of freedom that followed, not from any of her actions but from the mere fact that she grew up and became big and strong. To try and take a middle position—i.e., Washoe is like a child, aware but not responsible—does not quite work because she is a full-grown creature with the complement of maturity that comes from life's passages. To treat her as an incomplete human is to miss the point that she is a chimp.

She is a chimp in human society, and thus not a complete chimp. Would she have bitten Pribram had she matured in Africa and met him on equal terms? The evidence seems to be that if humans show a modicum of patience and deference to chimp manners, they can enjoy relatively civil relations with chimps in the wild, though from what I gather, such encounters are never entirely without strain. Beyond an understanding of what is bad form in chimp society, the key to wild encounters is an acknowledgment of the chimp's prerogatives, an acknowledgment of its individuality and right to its territory. In such circumstances it might be possible to make a judgment that a particular chimp violated the norms of civilized encounters. A judgment such as this is impossible in the United States because an acknowledgment of the chimp's right to territory and freedom of action is impossible in the United States. And this is true not just for the Lemmons and Pribrams, but also for the Foutses and others who see themselves as protectors and companions of chimps. And in the absence of a context in which captive chimps might be understood as individuals, they inevitably end up being treated as property.

However, because the chimp is in captivity, that does not mean it loses its own desire for respect and liberty, and this in turn makes the chimp an animal which, though it might be taught sign language and a host of other human activities, still cannot be domesticated. This means that the chimp will do things that seem to confirm the judgment that it is a wild animal, undeserving of rights and liberties.

The irony of all this is that Washoe, by biting Pribram, contributed in some measure to the melancholy fate of her peers. Still, she can't be held to blame. Nor does her behavior reflect on her intellectual capacities. She may have acted from time to time like a "wild and dangerous animal," but so do many people.

Roger himself has acknowledged the inevitable problems of captivity. At different points he explored the idea of bringing Washoe to Africa and habilitating her to the wild. He even contacted Janis Carter to see whether she would be interested in taking Washoe. (Janis demurred in part because of Washoe's reputation and in part because she was afraid that she would not be able to control a full-grown chimp with whom she had no prior relationship.)

The world in which Washoe and other sign-language-using chimps might be seen as creatures entitled to the rights and protections of humanity was like a soap bubble floating above a sea of spears. The notion might be tolerated so long as it did not collide with any of the myriad facets of the traditional view of their place in nature. While the notion might survive the first encounters with the scientific and philosophical establishment, when the proposition became one of economics, this fragile bubble did not have a chance.

The scientific climate affected the economic climate of the institute to be sure, but once the fate of the chimps became a question of economics, the fact that at one time they had appeared to be capable of conversing with human beings became immaterial. Thus, once the university cut the funding for the institute, Lemmon had to dispose of almost all the chimps who remained. The alternatives open for Booee, Bruno, Ally, Nim, Thelma, and the others were at best grim.

The alternatives were grim because without the protective noumena of language, the chimps were property, and property is not always treated well despite the best intentions.

If there was one bright spot in this gloomy picture for sign-language-using apes, it was surely the story of Koko, who thrived under the protection of the fiercely possessive Penny Patterson. But I was to discover that the very fierceness of Penny's protection had its own price, both for Penny and for Koko.

CHAPTER NINE

Penny and Ron and Koko and Michael

DURING the period in the late 1970s when Janis Carter was struggling to coax Lucy into chimpdom, and Roger Fouts and William Lemmon were working toward their endgame, I was preoccupied with another ape. This was the lowland gorilla Koko, who was the pupil of Penny Patterson. I got involved with Koko through happenstance. When I was researching my book *Apes, Men, and Language* in 1972–73, Penny was just getting started in her work with Koko. Then, in 1976, the *Encyclopaedia Britannica* asked me to write a feature about the sign-language experiments for the yearbook of their *Compton's Encyclopedia*. In the years since the publication of *Apes, Men, and Language*, I had heard a good deal about Koko, and so I took this opportunity to try to find out a bit more.

Of all the apes involved in language studies whom I have encountered over the years, Koko has moved about the least and has suffered the fewest dislocations. She was born in the San Francisco Zoo in 1971. Today she lives in the same trailer in which she spent her infancy, although in the intervening years that trailer has moved from San Francisco to Stanford University to Woodside, California. She currently lives within twenty miles of her birthplace. And since the first year of her life, she has had daily contact with Penny Patterson. However, despite this continuity, all is not rosy for Koko. To be sure, Penny Patterson is utterly dedicated to Koko, and I cannot imagine circumstances in which Penny would do anything other than devote all her energies to ensuring Koko's well-being. Nevertheless, over the years Penny and her partner Ron Cohen have gradually alienated themselves from virtually every institution and person that might help them. This alienation has been, in my view, unnecessary, and it is all the sadder because Koko is the most remarkable ape I have ever met. (I should note here that chimps, gorillas, and orangutans are all great apes, commonly referred to as apes.) Her future is threatened, not by the prospect of abandonment but rather by the very intensity of Penny's devotion.

My first meeting with Koko left me somewhat stunned. Watching Koko use Ameslan was entirely different from watching a chimpanzee engaged in the same process. Koko seemed more controlled and leisurely, more comfortable with the act of signing. In July 1976, Koko had just turned five. At that time, she was a solid ninety pounds—about a third of her present weight. Gorillas are perhaps the most beguiling apes of all. In a way they are just what you might expect them to be: hearty, confident, bemused, casual. Koko's signing then was precise (she has gotten sloppier as the years have gone by) and leisurely. I got the impression that she had integrated sign language to a great degree into her life.

It was as a graduate student in psychology at Stanford University that Penny Patterson became involved in sign-language work. She came to Stanford from the University of Illinois, where she had graduated with Phi Beta Kappa honors. It was there that she met Ron

Cohen, the electron-microscopy and recombinant-DNA specialist with whom she had lived since she came to California. Although not as well known to the public as Penny, Ron Cohen has been a key figure in Penny's life and work.

At the time of my first visit, Koko was living in her trailer, which was installed in a yard next to Stanford University's lab animal facility. The trailer had several rooms and an entranceway that were isolated from the rest of the space by wire mesh and gates. When I first arrived, Koko was waiting in her wire-enclosed playroom. She was told that I was a friend, a sign made by alternately locking the forefingers of the hands with one finger, then the other on top. She peered at me and then signed, "Please friend open hurry." The pace and clarity of her signing were entirely different from what I had seen in chimps. I think now that perhaps part of the difference is that the high energy level of chimps creates a background noise that influences our perceptions of their signing, and that because gorillas are much calmer animals, the background noise is reduced and the animal's signing seems that much clearer. So far, there has really not been a meaningful comparison of gorilla and chimp sign-language use that could lead to a definitive statement that one species is better at it than the other, but even knowing that, my own impression is that the richness and variety of Koko's signing was substantially more impressive than anything I had observed or read about in chimps.

After the initial introductions, I was let into Koko's playroom. She gave me a skeptical once-over, and then, apparently deciding that I was an OK kind of guy, she asked me in sign language to give her a "hard spin." Penny explained that this is a game in which Koko lies on her back and is spun around by the foot at the highest possible number of RPMs.

Thus began an intermittent relationship with Koko, characterized by a fair amount of rough and tumble, that

continued for the next four years. Koko even gave me a
name, "Arm," after our first few meetings. What happened was that the year after I wrote my article for
Compton's, Penny asked me if I would be interested in
working with her on a book. The idea appealed to me
because it offered the opportunity to approach the subject of ape language much more anecdotally than I had in
Apes, Men, and Language, and it appealed to me because I was so impressed by Koko.

And so I entered into collaboration with Penny to
write a book about Koko, a collaboration which ultimately produced *The Education of Koko*, published in
1981. After the book was finished, I was irritated by a
couple of actions initiated by Penny and Ron. As of this
writing I have not had any contact with Penny or Koko
for three years. I mention these circumstances in the interest of full disclosure, and because Penny's personality
and the way in which she has dealt with the world profoundly affect both Koko and the way she is perceived in
the scientific community.

During the period I worked on *The Education of
Koko*, I made several trips to California to research the
book. The trips averaged several weeks in length. During
the days I would plow through Penny's data and files and
then frequently stop in at the trailer to talk to Penny and
to play and talk with Koko. Shortly after my first visit,
Penny acquired two other gorillas, King Kong and Bebe.
Bebe died shortly after arrival from pneumonia brought
on by the rigors of the trip. Penny released the male
infant gorilla from the burden of the name King Kong
and renamed him Michael. Michael at that time weighed
only about forty pounds, but he had enormous hands,
which foreshadowed the size he would eventually grow
to. After he overcame his fear of Koko, the two would
roughhouse in the playroom, creating a titanic din.

During the course of my work with Penny, a number
of things happened which had the effect of dampening
my enthusiasm—not for Koko's facility with language

but rather for the way in which Penny and Ron had decided to deal with the scientific community and with the very publicity they had earlier courted. In sum, I quickly came to notice a bunker mentality in Penny and Ron, and it was not long before I began to believe that it was this bunker mentality that was the biggest obstacle to a true appreciation of the extraordinary things Koko was doing and saying.

To my mind, this mentality surfaced in a number of ways: in Ron's frequent and often vitriolic excommunications of people and institutions that he thought had slighted them in some way; in Penny and Ron's refusal to grant access to Koko or Penny's data to anyone who was not in a position to help them in some material way; and in the way in which Penny refused to share the glory with any of her assistants or allow them to develop their own research. The frustrating thing was that both Penny and Ron are enormously intelligent, and when they were not feeling beleaguered, they could be warm, witty, perceptive, and thoroughly charming.

Still, none of this matters in the long run, except insofar as it has affected Penny's ability to pursue and disseminate her work, and insofar as it has affected Koko's life. And it has affected both. Today the attitude of the scientific community toward Koko ranges from mystification or skepticism to the belief, on the part of a small group, that most of the accomplishments claimed for Koko are not authentic. This small group consists of some of the people who have visited Koko and observed the way in which she uses sign language.

Koko has been the subject of a number of short films and television programs, but because of the circumstances required for filming—camera crews, lights, equipment—these segments do not really capture what Koko is like. The films I have seen have shown numerous promptings and cuings on Penny's part and leave the false impression that Penny has to drag signs out of Koko. This could not be further from the truth, and so it is only those who have visited Koko in less stressful circumstances who have seen the real Koko.

Visitors see a gorilla who uses her several-hundred-word vocabulary to tell stories, escape blame, make jokes, tell fibs, understand her surroundings, and relate to her human and gorilla companions. Examples of Koko's wit are legion and have been widely cited. Most of her jokes seem to be attempts to sabotage what Koko considers to be boring drills and conversations. For instance, if Koko is bored or feeling obstreperous, she will vary the way a sign is made and, in so doing, subtly change its meaning. Once when asked too many times to make the "drink" sign (which is made by placing to the lips a thumb extended from a closed fist), Koko responded by making the sign in her ear. Another time, when shown bottles, she made the appropriate sign on her nose and then signed, "Funny there." On another occasion, when asked by an assistant whether she wanted food in her mouth, Koko replied, "Nose," precipitating the following conversation:

CINDY: Nose?
KOKO: Fake mouth.
CINDY: Where's your fake mouth?
KOKO: Nose.

This is just one of the hundreds of conversations Koko has carried on over the years, all recorded in the various logs Penny and her parade of assistants maintain, some of them also documented during Penny's own intermittent videotaping sessions. But few of these conversations have been published, and those that have are regarded with skepticism. Koko simply has not had the impact that she should have had.

One of the reasons for this became apparent to me during the research for *The Education of Koko*. Not long after the start of the project, the amount of signing by

Koko seemed to me to overwhelm Penny's capacity to digest and analyze it. She maintained a number of systems, ranging from daily logs to checklists for signs being stressed during a given month which were to be annotated, one-hour samples in which everything said and done by human and chimp was recorded, sessions in which everything was recorded on audio tape, videotaping sessions, and testing sessions of various sorts. In the course of these activities, Project Koko was generating paper at a rate that would leave the most dedicated bureaucrat lost in admiration. The problem was that most of this data was raw, in the sense that it had not been vetted except insofar as it pertained to Penny's thesis and to a few publications. I found it frustrating to work my way through the diaries because the marginalia which Penny and others had scribbled in to help them reconstruct the context on some later occasion were nearly useless to me. Moreover, there were vast files of data that had not been sorted.

Later, courtesy of the eminent logician Patrick Suppes, Penny was able to use the Stanford computers to help her manage her data, and she began to be able to impose some order on her data collection. For instance, various assistants would have directed conversations with Koko in which they would focus on particular themes or simply ask Koko questions, saying to her, for example, "You tell me!" Penny and others would go through the records of these conversations and sort the more interesting ones into separate files, in which the context would be explicated. This system was exceptionally helpful in my work on the book because it gave me a rare glimpse of the way in which Koko related to people when Penny was not around. On the other hand, while this file produced a rich store of anecdotal material, it was not producing anything on which Penny could base a scientific judgment of one sort or another.

Consequently Penny found herself forever in the position of citing Koko's more dramatic utterances and doings and then saying or writing variants of "We are in the process of analyzing the data to see whether..." or "We are in the process of accumulating evidence..." To date I have not seen or read about any of these substantiating analyses being published. This is understandable to a degree since, as Chris O'Sullivan points out, it is hard to publish while you have the ape on your hands.

The result is catastrophic in terms of credibility—not because of what Koko can or cannot do but because the context of the scientific debate is so far removed from the sophisticated behaviors that Penny attributes to her. While Penny claims Koko has made rhymes in English and sign language, Sebeok and his crowd are roaming the country saying apes do not even understand words as symbols. Those of us who have seen Koko do these and other remarkable things cannot point to any formal studies documenting the behaviors (if in fact it is possible to construct a test with adequate controls for humor, lying, rhyming, and the like); the scientific community has access to neither Penny or her data.

In truth, I sympathize with Penny for not wanting to open her work to people like Sebeok and Terrace. Having someone tour the country saying that you are a fraud before they have even visited your experiment does not create a desire to have them visit your experiment. (At the indictment of language work with apes that Sebeok staged during his 1980 conference on Clever Hans at the New York Academy of Sciences, one of his colleagues, the Amazing Randi, talked about seeing outright cuing in a videotape of an incident in which Koko had a dispute about the color of her blanket. I pointed out that the particular incident had occurred when Koko was alone with Barbara Hiller and had never been videotaped.) On the other hand, even Terrace has made a small part of his data available to his critics (and, as noted, some of them have used it to dispute *his* findings), and for Penny to husband her data so closely implies to those who do not know her that she has something to hide.

This impression is compounded by the fact that Penny has on occasion stretched her interpretations of Koko's gestures. For instance, one of the differences between Project Washoe and Project Koko is that Penny allowed gestures in which Koko pointed to a part of the body to be counted as words, while the Gardners did not. Penny asserts that pointing to one's eye is an acceptable way of saying "eye" in Ameslan. The Gardners don't disagree, but they still did not count such clearly iconic gestures as words. On a number of occasions, Penny has cited a statement in which Koko referred to body parts as an example of Koko's using her vocabulary to make a point about something which had nothing to do with her vocabulary. The example had to do with Koko's boredom with constant drills involving naming body parts—one of the first things that a new assistant would do during initial sessions with Koko. When asked what was boring by one such assistant, Koko responded, "Think eye ear eye nose boring." The statement makes perfect sense when considered in the context of a number of Koko's other statements and her known displeasure with drills. It's really pretty funny.

But when you examine what the actual gestures looked like, the statement seems less dramatic. "Think" is made by tapping the side of the forehead. The "eye," "ear," and "nose" signs are made by simply pointing to each of the features. Thus the first five gestures in the statement all consist of tapping or pointing to parts of the head in close succession. "Boring" is made by feigning a yawn or by twisting a finger (apes tend to tap rather than twist) into the side of the nose, and so the entire statement involves moving the hands about the face. Koko can be very precise in signing, but she can also be sloppy, and she has huge hands. The point is that Penny's interpretation of this particular statement is problematic. A number of scientists have told me that it is precisely this lack of caution that so infuriates her colleagues. By retelling this and a few other problematical statements over and over Penny gives critics an opportunity to undermine the general credibility of Koko's statements.

On several occasions, Penny has cited some of Michael's statements, which she interprets as referring to his capture in the wild. I did not think that we should mention these in our book because she could offer little evidence to support her conclusions. However, Penny has related this story and her interpretation of it to a number of people, as well as in the newsletter she publishes. I assume that this story influenced Michael Crichton in the writing of *Congo*, which revolves around a sign-language-using gorilla who remembers her infancy in the jungle.

The story may well be true, but that Penny so enthusiastically promotes this interpretation does not enhance her credibility among the skeptical. Penny seems to have decided "damn the critics, full speed ahead." It is another manifestation of the bunker mentality: if people choose not to believe her, that is their problem, not hers. She has Koko, and she knows how bright Koko is.

Even with this attitude, Penny might still prevail in the court of credibility if she were to encourage students and assistants to develop their own relationships with Koko and Michael and to develop their own research. Penny was always saying that this was precisely what she wanted. Yet she has had a procession of assistants who have arrived starry-eyed with anticipation and have left more or less disillusioned. Part of the problem is that at present Penny has no affiliation with a university, and so there is no natural source of graduate students and assistants. When I was working on our book in the late 1970s, Penny's often stormy relationship with Stanford was coming to an end, and both she and Ron seemed to like the idea of establishing themselves independently of a university. The other part of the problem is that either consciously or unconsciously Penny and Ron did not seem to want others to develop strong relationships with the gorillas.

I noticed that on several occasions when I found some particularly telling example of signing elicited by one of Penny's assistants, she would come back a few days later with a "better" example that *she* had elicited. These and other actions created a situation in which the assistants were left with little in the way of incentives. Penny had almost no money, and so she could not pay more than nominal wages. On the other hand, the assistants were expected to show the same dedication that Penny and Ron demonstrated. The assistants quickly discovered that working with the gorillas was not going to enhance their own studies or careers. Without these incentives, the work quickly becomes drudgery no matter how fond they might be of Koko and Michael. Working on Project Koko became for many assistants a way station rather than the start of a career, and in consequence Project Koko never developed the cadre of academically influential alumni who could write and help spread the word about Koko's accomplishments.

One final piece of fallout from Penny and Ron's attitude, I think, has been its effects on Koko's relationship with Penny. Unlike the other sign-language-using apes, Koko has never left home and hearth. And the way Penny has chosen to relate to the world has only reinforced her role as the primary figure in Koko's life and vice versa. Their relationship has all the overlays of love, bickering, and resentment of the relationship between a mother and daughter who have spent their lives closeted together in some isolated Appalachian town. Were Koko human, their life together might have been a fitting subject for treatment by Tennessee Williams. Koko and Penny know each other so well that merely to read a transcript of their signing conversations is to glimpse only a very small portion of the interplay between them. I am not referring here to the question of cuing; rather I am referring to agendas Koko and Penny bring to their meetings that have nothing to do with the scientific side of Penny's work. This is why I was so interested in the conversations that the assistants had had with Koko.

The depth of Koko and Penny's relationship and of Penny's immersion in the world of signing gorillas probably contributes to her lack of caution in offering what to other people might seem stretched interpretations of Koko's and Michael's signs. The gorillas are her world, and it is a world she can understand and control.

Penny's newsletter notes that she has found land in Hawaii where she might finally give the gorillas the freedom to live in a setting that more closely approximates their natural home. She is trying to raise several million dollars, and I wish her well in the endeavor. Although Penny may infuriate her colleagues, she has done wonders for the image of gorillas in the public mind. More particularly I would love to see Koko and Michael liberated from the confines of their present home.

Man Bites Chimp

CHAPTER TEN

The Chimp Glut

THE GOOD days of the Institute for Primate Studies in the early to mid-1970s shortly preceded what might be called a golden age for captive chimpanzees. A growing appreciation of the behavioral communalities of ape and human, recognition of the animal's endangered status, and a resurgent interest in the rights of animals led to pressures for improved care of chimps and temporary protection from use in "terminal" studies that are the stock-in-trade of laboratory research. To a degree this temporary enlightenment reflected the brief glory of the sign-language experiments. There were even pressures from within such redoubts of vivisection as the National Institutes of Health to draw up new guidelines governing the care and use of chimpanzees in medical research. Until Ronald Reagan was elected, there was the promise that the future for captive chimps might prove better than it had formerly been.

It was not that Ronald Reagan had anything against chimpanzees but rather that the bleak future for federal funding for research changed the context within which laboratories and research facilities looked at their popu-

lations of chimpanzees, particularly their populations of
adult male chimps.

Chimps are popular in medical research. The reason
is that genetically they are so similar to humans that in a
number of respects chimp and human anatomy and immune systems are virtually indistinguishable. If science
is uncomfortable acknowledging behavioral continuities
with man, it has no qualms about acknowledging our biological brotherhood with chimps, particularly since this
allows researchers to do things to apes that are considered too dangerous to try with humans. Like the me-
chanic son of a patrician family, their kinship is
acknowledged when something breaks down, and otherwise they are treated as something of an embarrassment.
Thus it was that a chimp named Ham (now dead) made
the first American space flight, playing Tenzing to Alan
Shepard's Sir Edmund Hillary. I have heard it asserted
several times that we would not have the polio vaccine
were it not for elaborate, sometimes terminal studies
done on chimpanzees. "Terminal" means that the study
entails the death of the animal in order that its corpse
may be studied.

According to Alfred Prince, author of a study on the
research use of chimpanzees done for the National Institutes of Health, "...biologically it would appear that
chimpanzees differ from man little more than one man
does from another. Chimpanzee chromosomes...are almost identical to those of man.... Several proteins are
so similar that when human serum is repeatedly injected
into chimpanzees...anti-normal serum protein antibod-
ies are only rarely produced....Moreover type A red
blood cells survive normally when transfused into chimpanzees with type A blood....Clearly, the biochemical
and immunologic data provide little basis for separation
of these species."

At first this might seem cause for celebration: we can
welcome chimps to the club that we have invented for
ourselves at the supposed pinnacle of evolution. Reading

a little further in Prince's study, one discovers, however, that this close kinship with man makes the chimp ideal for studies of hepatitis, tumor virus, parasitology, and such viruses as kuru (Carl Gajdusek won the Nobel prize for his analysis of this disease in a study which reportedly involved killing 125 chimpanzees), which involve the slow degeneration of the central nervous system. Because of their kinship with us, chimps are also used in very dangerous research in experimental surgery, toxicology, and pharmacology. Today there are a number of studies under way that seek to determine whether chimps can acquire AIDS; if they can, then the disease will be able to be more thoroughly studied in chimps than in human beings. Given the rewards chimps have reaped for this kinship with man, they might be forgiven if they said "No, thanks" to all this evidence of brotherhood and sought to have themselves classified with the lizards.

Still, until the last couple of years, chimps were somewhat protected from cavalier sacrifice on the altar of medicine. The climate has changed because a growing glut of captive male chimpanzees makes the temptation to find an economically sound "use" for the animals irresistible. Females are valuable for their breeding potential. On the other hand, adult males are too big and strong and proud to be used in behavioral or other research that requires contact with an unsedated animal, and once they have been used in most nonfatal medical studies, they are useless for most other medical studies. This is because most studies require chimps with a clean and known epidemiological history. Inevitably people who run research labs begin to wonder what they are going to do with these animals, who might live fifty years and who cost between fifteen and thirty dollars a day to feed, house, and care for. The problem is constantly compounded because there is great demand for infant chimpanzees in all sorts of medical and behavioral studies. Infants are easy to work with, and they have known medical histories. As laboratories get better and better at breeding chimpanzees, they create future adult male chimps at an ever-increasing rate. There are now roughly 1,700 captive chimps in the United States, and since most of them are far younger than a chimp's maximum age, the population increases at roughly the birth rate (about 80 a year at the moment) minus those killed by disease, accident, and medical study. I do not know whether any laboratory chimp has yet died of natural causes, and it becomes increasingly unlikely that any laboratory chimp will live to enjoy that luxury.

The stage was thus set for a new dark age for captive male chimps. Endangered in the wild, in the early 1980s they were equally endangered in our laboratories, ironically because of their growing numbers in captivity. One longtime chimp specialist said to me, "If it hasn't happened yet, I can guarantee you that by this time next year, someone will have put a few of these chimps to death." Regrettably he was right.

This was the climate in which Lemmon began to address the question of what to do with his chimp colony in the absence of sufficient funds to keep it going. It must be said that he took great pains to try to find a place where his colony might stay together and not be subject to medical research or testing. In the end, he had to make do with a compromise destiny for his chimps, sign-language-using and otherwise. And this compromise catapulted the institute and its inmates back into the headlines.

CHAPTER ELEVEN

Man
Bites Chimp

IT WAS spring of 1982, in effect, the Prague Spring for the ape language experiments. Things were beginning to look better for a couple of the apes. Penny had received a generous infusion of funds from a donor, with which she was able to improve the facilities for the gorillas in Woodside, and Washoe and Loulis were comfortably ensconced in Ellensburg, Washington, while Roger Fouts took occasional leaves to advise the makers of the movie *Greystoke*. However, this sunniness did not extend to the Institute for Primate Studies. William Lemmon was in the process of shipping off the adult chimp colony; the university had informed him that funding for the institute would be cut off in July, and he was hurrying to beat the deadline.

Lemmon had made his decision about where he would send the chimps the previous fall. At the time there were no objections from any of the people who had been involved with Ally, Nim, Booee, Bruno, or the rest of the colony. This was principally because most of those who had worked closely with those apes were cut off from the institute. Moreover, the story as it filtered out of the institute kept changing. People would hear that the apes were not being sold, that they were only being loaned out, or that Lemmon had sold them, but with all sorts of restrictions on how they might be used.

However, during that fateful spring, Chris O'Sullivan got a phone call from a woman who still worked with Lemmon. Chris was surprised because she and the woman had earlier had a falling out. To explain why she was calling, Chris remembers, the woman said, "This time Lemmon's done something I just can't forgive," and she went on to outline the sale of the chimps to a medical laboratory. Chris became upset when she learned of Ally's destiny. After some soul-searching, she called an aunt, Jane Schulberg, who worked for CBS. The aunt passed the word to CBS News, which then sent Steve Kroft, a correspondent who had just returned from El Salvador, to cover the story. Kroft flew up from Texas with a camera crew to visit Lemmon and at first decided that the story was a tempest in a teapot. Before he left, he called Chris (who had no idea that her telephone call had had any effect). With some irritation he said, "I've just come back from El Salvador. Now tell me why I should care about a few chimpanzees." Chris told him.

On the strength of their conversation, Kroft decided not to leave Oklahoma just yet. Chris went out to meet Kroft near the airport and suggested that Kroft call a few other people before catching his plane. As he made these calls, Kroft began to see that perhaps there was, after all, a story in the chimps. Ultimately CBS ran a piece about the movement of the chimps. In network terms it was not a short item. It involved the basic information as well as brief interviews with Roger Fouts, Herb Terrace, and James Mahoney of the medical laboratory, and it had considerable effect.

Lemmon suddenly found himself in the midst of a cause célèbre. People who had not objected when Lemmon first discussed the chimps' fate suddenly rose in high dudgeon to denounce the move. Herbert Terrace, never shy about appearing on network television, conveniently forgot that he had known about the move for several months and announced that he was going to file a lawsuit to save Nim. Animal rights groups of all stripes entered the fray, condemning Lemmon's move and proposing various alternatives. For a few weeks in that spring, virtually every possible perspective on the relationship of man and chimp was expressed by some group offering an opinion on what was going on. The only thing that was ignored was reality.

The cause of this clamor was that sign-language-using chimps were being sold to a place called LEMSIP—Laboratory for Experimental Medicine and Surgery in Primates. The very name raised the spectre of Ally and Nim having limbs hacked off by researchers testing new techniques in surgical reattachment. Given the transient nature of press coverage, the first version of a story is quite often the version that gets enshrined in the popular mind. I must admit that when I first heard about Lemmon's decision (a few months before the brouhaha), I was alarmed as well. My immediate alarm about the chimps being sent to LEMSIP was very quickly put to rest by conversations with the people who run it. The chimps are not going to be sawed up—at least not while present management is there. The laboratory is run on a day-to-day basis primarily by Dr. James Mahoney, a man who is sincerely dedicated to the welfare of chimpanzees. Still, the chimps have been used in the testing of hepatitis B vaccines, and the economic pressures mentioned in the previous chapter represent a continuing threat to their future. Whether or not the immediate concerns of those aroused by the publicity about Lemmon's decision were misplaced, the image of trucks laden with veterans of sign-language experiments lumbering off to the medical lab is not a happy one.

The controversy broke shortly after I returned from

visits to Oklahoma and LEMSIP in April and May of 1982. Here are the events as I saw them unfold.

I went out to Oklahoma in April of 1982 to check into the situation. I had heard from Roger Fouts several months earlier that there was trouble at the institute. By the time I got out to Oklahoma in April, Booee, Bruno, and a few other chimps had already been moved to LEMSIP. Ally, Nim, and a number of other chimps had not yet made the move. The weather was bright and warm, and Oklahoma was alive with the breath of flowers and shrubs enjoying those few transitional weeks before they would be baked by the summer sun. Despite the promise of the weather, the institute had a sad, run-down look to it, as though its spirit had been depleted by the successive departures of Roger, the graduate students, and now the chimps. The island where a language-using chimp colony was to have been installed was overgrown, the rowboat which had figured in both chimp pranks and Washoe's famous use of "water bird" to describe a swan lay in slimy neglect, beached by the receding waters of the moat. The cages in the main colony looked dirty and worn. The only cheerful spot in this gloom was a spanking-clean nursery Lemmon had constructed since my last visit. Whatever happens to the adult chimp colony, Dr. Lemmon intends to maintain a small group in order to continue to breed chimps.

I went out to the institute with Chris O'Sullivan. After reacquainting myself with the layout, we went in to visit Ally. I had had only fleeting glimpses of Ally in the previous years, and it was hard to reconcile this big male with the scholarly-looking, freckle-faced juvenile chimp I remembered. Upon seeing us Ally started to work himself up into an aggressive display, to which Chris responded by saying to him, "Oh, Ally, you don't have to do that with us." Apparently seeing the logic of Chris's remark, Ally broke off the theatrics and came over to hunker down by the bars. By all accounts, no one had signed with Ally for years, and so I was not sure what to expect. In his youth, Ally had been something of a star in Ameslan studies. Chris decided to lead things off by seeing whether he remembered me. "Who he?" she signed, pointing at me. Ally did not venture an answer, although he stared at me intently. Then Chris said, "What do you want?" Ally promptly signed, "Key." Chris asked the same question again. This time, Ally signed, "Food." Then after some more small talk, Chris began bringing out objects and asking Ally what they were—a watch, glasses, a shoe. Ally responded crisply and accurately, occasionally interrupting the proceedings to ask for a "drink" or a "cup." We may well have cued Ally, and there was certainly nothing scientific about this conversation, but Ally seemed to relish it and the chance to use his sign language to communicate. Before we left, Chris again asked Ally who I was. This time he signed, "Person."

From the main colony we walked over to the shed to visit Nim, who was sharing quarters with the female chimp Vanessa. It did not look as if the relationship was much of a success. When we showed up, Vanessa trampled Nim to get near us as Nim huddled in a corner. Nim was reluctant to sign at first, but after being asked what he wanted a few times, he signed, "Food," then, "Drink," and then, "Key."

The next day something strange happened. I again went to the institute, this time with Laurie MacIvor, a zoologist who had spent a good deal of time at the institute in the early days of the sign-language experiments. In contrast to the day before, Ally showed no hesitation in signing. He rushed up to the bars and answered all our questions. Laurie went over to visit Jezzabel, whom she had worked with years before. Laurie reported that during their chat, Jezzie made the signs "eat," "drink," "berry," "key," and "hat." Laurie noted that she had made a point of visiting Jezzie every year, and that this was the first time since the work had ended that she had seen her make more than a sloppy "eat" sign. She also reported that another chimp, MacArthur, had joined in the conversation by making the signs "eat" and "key." All this activity was striking because, according to Lemmon, it had been years since the chimps had had any regular exposure to sign language.

Of course there is no way of knowing definitively what this increase in signing means, but I was intrigued by what Laurie said about Jezzabel. We had no rewards to offer on any of our visits. Had the fact that after so many years a couple of people were interested in signing somehow spread excitement through the chimp colony? It is true that the signing we initiated and witnessed was confined to rather rudimentary topics, such as food and the possibility of escape, but I left with the feeling that sign language was an important means of contact with humanity for these chimps. It must be somewhat mystifying to them that no one seems to care about communicating with them in this way anymore. Even though virtually all sign contact with any of the chimps ceased long ago, the chimps themselves have not given up signing. What do the signs mean to these chimps? Why did they enter into signing again with such alacrity? At the time of my visit, no one was really interested in finding out the answers to these questions. Roger Fouts was gone, sign-language experiments were out of favor, and little funding was available, even if people had been interested in these questions. Only the chimps had not gotten the news.

It was during this trip to Oklahoma that I had a number of conversations with Lemmon about the circumstances of Roger's departure. We also spoke freely about LEMSIP and Lemmon's decision to sell the chimps to the lab. Although we had never crossed swords in the past, Lemmon perceived me to be a friend of Roger Fouts's, and in his opening remarks, he intimated that he had little hope of appearing in a favorable light in any version of our conversation that I might publish. The idea that I might not be in either Roger's or his camp would have been as strange to Lemmon as it would be to Roger (who also saw people in terms of whether they were with him or against him). Despite his skepticism with respect to my intentions, Lemmon was interested in explaining his position.

He began by discussing the alternatives. On the one hand, he wanted the colony kept together, and he wanted it preserved from laboratories and zoos (although he has in the past traded with zoos), and on the other, he did not think rehabilitation such as that being carried out by Janis Carter would work. "By the time a chimp gets to the age where he is to be sent back there [to Africa]," said Lemmon, "he is not a chimp anymore . . . it [rehabilitation] is a lovely idea, and it comforts the bleeding hearts."

Basically Lemmon said that a key part of his decision to sell the colony to LEMSIP was his respect for Jim Mahoney. "I trust him without equivocation," he said. He would have preferred that the chimps not be involved in any testing whatsoever, but he said "serum testing is harmless, and by the grace of God no hardship for the chimp." The serum testing that Lemmon referred to is the batch testing of hepatitis B vaccines, about which I will have more to say.

Lemmon spoke about the conditions he had imposed with respect to the sale, his desire to keep the colony together, and his interest in their long-term well-being. Nevertheless, conversations with other people involved in the transfer of the chimps led me to believe that there was little on paper governing the future disposition of the animals, and even if there had been, it quickly became clear that though Lemmon's stipulations might have sounded reassuring to him and to others concerned for the chimps' welfare, more powerful forces would determine the chimps' fate once they had left the institute.

As I drove away from the institute, one of the chimps watched the progress of my car. Looking back, I thought

I saw the chimp making a sign. But I might have been seeing things.

AFTER visiting LEMSIP and speaking with the people there, I found it hard either to condemn or to praise it. It is a well-tended facility in a very pretty part of New York State. The scientists and technicians who work there seemed to be well trained and dedicated. Quite a number of the technicians I spoke with had been there for several years, and all seemed genuinely interested in chimps. On the other hand, the cages, while scrupulously maintained, do not allow the freedom of movement available at the more primitive facility in Norman, Oklahoma. There is no large enclosure which will permit a large group of chimps to get together, although some of the cages do have interconnecting passageways. Nor is there anything to look at which might prove diverting to the chimps. The cage areas are all painted the same color, and the walls are undecorated. Despite the enlightenment of the people running the place, the facility is quite clearly administered as a medical laboratory and not as a home for chimps. This is confirmed by the fact that it was drug-company money which saved LEMSIP when it was on the point of being shut down two years ago.

One of the first people I spoke with at LEMSIP was Dr. Elizabeth Muchmore. She made the point that despite its name, LEMSIP has avoided hazardous research. In fact, she said, LEMSIP had turned down a gall-bladder study because the sponsoring organization wanted it to be terminal. As we shall see, things have changed at LEMSIP since she made that statement.

At the time when the signing chimps were sent from the institute to LEMSIP, no research at all was being done there. The chimps were being used in the batch testing of hepatitis B vaccine, and it was this testing that caused much alarm at first.

Hepatitis B is a prevalent chronic disease that does

not have the acute effects associated with hepatitis A but which quite often leads to liver cancer or cirrhosis. Estimates of the number of carriers range as high as two hundred million people. Although there are a number of uncomfortable symptoms associated with hepatitis B in human beings, they do not seem to affect chimps, who can also contract the disease. Dr. Elizabeth Muchmore said, "Hepatitis for a chimp is like a glass of water. They don't get sick." On the other hand, no one really knows what the long-term effects of giving hepatitis B to a chimp may be. It is not known, for instance, whether or not the disease will increase the likelihood that a chimp will get liver cancer. Dr. Muchmore noted that 5 to 10 percent of the chimps infected with the virus will become carriers of hepatitis B and that they will be likely to develop liver disease. But she added that Shirley, a carrier who was then twenty-three years old, still enjoyed fine health.

There are those who think that the benefits of using chimps as proxies in the study and testing of hepatitis vaccine far outweigh whatever potential hardships for chimps these studies entail. Said Elizabeth Muchmore, "In a way, this testing is how the chimps pay their dues to a society that is saving them from extinction." Alfred Prince, who runs a primate laboratory in Liberia, wrote the analysis of the use of primates in medical testing that I mentioned earlier; with regard to hepatitis B, he noted that as late as 1980 only one chimpanzee had died from hepatitis B infection. Prince wrote, ". . . it found there, fewer than 200 chimpanzees have been used for all hepatitis B-related studies. . . . these studies made possible the testing of a hepatitis B vaccine in man within 10 years of the discovery of a hepatitis B surface antigen—a truly remarkable achievement."

The tests themselves are relatively prosaic. The chimps are tranquilized to receive the hepatitis vaccine. Then they receive the virus by injection. Following this, they undergo periodic blood sampling, which determines whether the batch of vaccine in question worked or not. After six or nine months, the testing ends and the chimps are made available for other studies.

I visited LEMSIP several times. At the time of my first visit, Booee and Bruno, and several other less notable students of sign language, were there, but Ally and Nim had not yet been shipped. I returned for a second visit just a few days after Ally and Nim and a few companions had arrived.

On that first occasion, I looked in on Bruno and Booee. Taped to the front of their cages was a small sign. On the posted note were depictions of a number of Ameslan signs and their meanings. I was being taken around by Jerry Clause, a technician, who greeted Bruno in Ameslan as well as in English. Bruno asked Jerry for a cigar. Jerry mentioned to me that Bruno often asked for drinks, water, or a smoke.

I was a little taken aback, and when I spoke to Jim Mahoney later that day, I asked him whether the chimps signed. "Oh, they sign all the time," he said. "That's why we put up the posters. The technicians kept seeing the chimps make these gestures, and they wanted to be able to respond." Mahoney at first shared cigarettes with Booee when he asked for a smoke; however, he has since given up smoking. He says that he has tried to explain to Booee that if he carried cigarettes he would start smoking again, but that Booee seems unwilling to accept that excuse.

When Ally and Nim arrived, I took the opportunity to renew the conversations we had had in Oklahoma. "What do you want?" I asked. Ally first signed, "Drink," then, "Food." Then he got excited: "More food . . . more fruit," and finally, "Hurry more fruit." At this point, Ally had only been at LEMSIP three days, and he was clearly anxious about his surroundings. I don't doubt that he remembered me from Oklahoma. Perhaps asking for food was a way of asking for reassurance that everything was going to be all right—in much the same way that certain rituals of hospitality address similar anxieties in the non-Western world. Or perhaps these were the only signs that Ally could get a response to among the technicians, whose vocabularies were limited to the words on the few signs posted on the cages.

What was clear was that Ally was very concerned about his new home, and being concerned, he had resorted to the gestural language he had been taught as a means of communicating with human beings. In his recent life, however, fewer and fewer people either knew sign language or used it with him, and as in so many other cases, it must have seemed somewhat strange to Ally that this means of communication was gradually becoming archaic.

Jim Mahoney was interested enough in the gestures to acquire a few signs so that he would know what the chimps were talking about; however, Mahoney is a longtime student of chimp behavior, and he feels that he can express subtleties using chimp gestures, vocalizations, and shadings that neither he nor the chimps could begin to express in sign language.

I have no reason to doubt that this is true for Jim Mahoney, and it seems that without people fluent in Ameslan and willing to converse, the ambit of chimp conversation diminishes. However, it is very hard to determine what that diminution means, because my impression is that almost no one in recent years has either spent the time or possessed the vocabulary to get past the level of basic amenities.

This, then, is the chimp colony's life at LEMSIP. They suffer certain penalties that derive from their being man's closest relative, but they are in the hands of people who are sensitive to their needs—including their need to communicate in the language they have been taught. Had they not enjoyed earlier celebrity, the story would not even have merited a mention on the news services. After all, chimps are being bought and sold all the time. Once they have acquired sign language, it becomes

clear that the sale of these animals to a medical laboratory is far from being a simple financial transaction. Suddenly the issue involves emotions stirred by our
sensitivity to the fragile species barrier. How important
these emotions are became clear when the CBS story
ran, and the chimps found themselves once again in the
spotlight.

CHAPTER TWELVE

A Momentary Anger

BETWEEN my first and second trips to LEMSIP, I watched on TV the CBS news item on the sale of the signing chimps. There was Herb Terrace expressing shock and dismay over the fate of Nim. He said he had no idea that Nim was about to be sold to LEMSIP, and he said that while it was true that Nim had not learned a language, he was a highly sensitive and social creature, who deserved better than a medical lab. When I returned to LEMSIP, Jim Mahoney told me that several months before the CBS item, Terrace had called Jo and Paul Fritz, of the Primate Foundation of Arizona, to see whether they would take Nim so he wouldn't have to go to LEMSIP. Mahoney knew this because he knew someone who happened to be in the room when the Fritzes were talking with Terrace on the telephone. In other words, according to Mahoney, despite Terrace's expressions of surprise about the destiny of Nim, he had known about where Nim was going for several months.

The news item on television precipitated a whole

series of follow-up stories, and these stories in turn got
various animal rights groups interested in the fate of the
chimps. At different times, the *Washington Post*, the
New York Times, and the *Village Voice*, among other
newspapers and magazines, ran major stories on the
movements of the chimps. (After the fray died down, I
wrote an article that was published in the *New York
Times Magazine*.) The Humane Society, Cleveland
Amory's Fund for Animals, and People for the Ethical
Treatment of Animals were galvanized into action. Jim
Mahoney of LEMSIP found himself and the director of
the laboratory, Dr. Jan Moor-Jankowski, cast as villains
in the affair.

Ally, Nim, MacArthur, and a few other cohorts were
delivered to LEMSIP on June 5. On June 9, Robert
Reinhold wrote an article in the *Times* which detailed the
growing storm over the animals. The situation was very
confusing. Terrace, with his newly minted outrage, was
promoting Lion Country Safari in Florida as an alternative retirement home for Ally and Nim. The Humane
Society announced (prematurely, as it turned out) that
the chimps would be going to Primarily Primates, a private refuge outside San Antonio. Not mentioned in the
article were Cleveland Amory's offer to buy Nim and
house him at Black Beauty Ranch, the Fund for Animals
refuge for abused horses in Texas, or the offer by Francine Neago (Neago is a Frenchwoman living in California who has a longtime interest in the great apes) to
house Ally outside of Los Angeles, or another plan, proposed by Bob Ingersoll and Alysse Moor, who had been
Lemmon's administrative assistant, to set up Nim and a
few other chimps on a chicken ranch which Moor and
Ingersoll's father could buy. Alysse Moor already had
custody of one chimp, Lily, whose plight had caused her
to join forces with Ingersoll. Ultimately she sent Lily to
Francine Neago when it became clear that the chimp colony was to be sold. The Ingersoll-Moor proposal was
particularly interesting because among the other behav-

ioral studies they hoped to pursue was a further evalua-
tion of Nim's abilities with sign language.

While these alternatives were being bandied about,
LEMSIP found itself under continuous attack. A letter
to the *New York Post* spoke of consigning Ally and Nim
to a lingering death, and Mahoney found himself the recipient of abusive phone calls and letters. Even such no-
tables as Jane Goodall got into the act. She wrote the
president of the University of Oklahoma, deploring the
fact that animals who had been raised as part of families
"... will be subjected to life imprisonment and, in all
probability, much pain and fear."

The weight of this outcry was such that both New
York University (which owned LEMSIP and which was
being picketed by people protesting the sale of the
chimps) and the University of Oklahoma decided that
the negative publicity about Ally and Nim was far more
costly than the expense of sending the two celebrity
chimps back to Oklahoma while their fate was being decided. Thus the two chimps, whose previous movement
was dictated largely by economics, found their return
trip dictated by humanitarian, or, more precisely, public
relations motives. The outcry had forged a new context
within which to view the animals. The fact that here
were animals who could say "out" and "no" gave animal
rights groups an irresistible lever in the whole question
of medical experimentation on animals. And, in fact, it is
hard to find fault with the capacity for empathy with our
fellow creatures that this crisis brought into the open.

As is the case with so many public causes, emotions
admirable in themselves blinded people to the reality of
the chimps' situation; and to this day it is unclear
whether the outcome actually hurt the chimps while
salving consciences. This was Jim Mahoney's feeling.
When I spoke to Jim Mahoney during this troubled period, he was not about to take sitting down all the criticism he was receiving. Mahoney, who was born in
Ireland and still retains enough of an accent to freight

each word with both challenge and significance, said, "I think it's a bit hypocritical. Sure, Ally and Nim are being taken care of, but what about the rest of the chimps who don't have famous names? If everybody who got up in arms about the chimps actually did something about it, we would have a much better facility. People send a telegram and think they've done something. What they don't understand is that in our 'wicked' way we are trying to do something every day."

Indeed, life went back to normal at LEMSIP once their notorious prisoners were shipped back to Oklahoma. Left behind were several other sign-language-using chimps, including Booee and Bruno, who did not have famous names, and who, as Mahoney had predicted, were quickly forgotten.

Moreover, once the chimps were returned from LEMSIP to Oklahoma, the energy went out of the outcry, and Ally and Nim's future was addressed with considerably less urgency and thought than went into the original decision to send them to LEMSIP. What happened to Ally in particular could hardly be said to have improved his circumstances over those at LEMSIP. At least at LEMSIP the handlers knew his name.

On November 15, 1982, Ally, who had been a good breeding male, was dispatched to do stud service at a private laboratory called White Sands Research Center. From this point onward, the fate of Ally is somewhat mysterious. Some reports hold that he did not adjust well and was shipped back to Oklahoma, but sources at White Sands assert that the two male breeding chimps that Buckshire delivered on November 19, 1982, are still there.

Checking the whereabouts of Ally has been complicated because of two circumstances. The Institute for Primate Studies is now all but defunct, and Dr. Lemmon has suffered a string of personal tragedies and health problems which have kept him from responding to requests for information. Pat Crown, who still works for

Lemmon, confirmed, however, that Ally was in the shipment that went to White Sands.

However, one other circumstance confuses the situation. According to Dr. William Cummins, the chief veterinarian at White Sands, computer records show that neither of the males received from Buckshire on November 19 was listed as having a name. Dr. Cummins was not at White Sands in 1982, and so he had no knowledge of why that should be, but White Sands has given the two breeding males from that shipment the names of Harry and Midge.

After repeated phone calls to Buckshire, which delivered the animals, I finally was told by one employee that Buckshire shipping records do not take note of the origin of the animals they ship. (Other primate facility officials told me that state permits do not allow the shipment of chimpanzees without noting their origin.) Officials at White Sands Research Center noted that neither of the males delivered that day was tattooed, which corresponds with the policy of the Institute for Primate Studies.

So Ally is in all probability Harry or Midge. No one I contacted at White Sands would admit to knowing about their charge's illustrious past, and clearly no one has signed to either of these chimps. At my request, Dr. Cummins asked the handlers whether they had ever noticed anything out of the ordinary in either chimp's behavior, and, according to Dr. Cummins, the answer was in the negative. When asked about them, Dr. Cummins noted that neither of them "has been worth a damn as a breeder." Ally was known to be a good breeder in Oklahoma, but it would not be unusual for a traumatic change to affect his breeding habits. It could be said that losing the name you have lived with for your entire life would be traumatic. At least at LEMSIP, the handlers knew Ally's name and would sign with him. For the past three years, it seems he has been a stranger surrounded by strangers.

Actually, Ally's disappearance into the realm of undocumented chimpdom is not so unusual when you consider that for the buyers and sellers of these animals, the chimp's epidemiological history is far more important than its name. But it is ironic that while Ally's trip to LEMSIP caused such a stir, his trip to White Sands Research Center went unremarked.

Nim was a different case. Dr. Lemmon was in no mood for any more of Terrace's posturings, and he dismissed his attempts to buy Nim back. Forgetting that six years earlier he had shipped Nim prematurely back to the institute to get him off his hands, Terrace told the *Village Voice*, "We stand here with our hands out wanting to buy these chimps, but nobody will sell them to us." Early in 1983, a deal was struck between the institute and Cleveland Amory's group, the Fund for Animals, and Nim was shipped off to Black Beauty Ranch in Texas. It is unclear how Nim is adapting to Black Beauty Ranch, but it must be pointed out that the facility was never intended for chimps, and in fact Nim was the only chimp there. (I should point out that about a year after Nim arrived at Black Beauty Ranch, the Fund for Animals obtained a female companion for Nim, a former circus chimp named Sally. The two are still together.) Chimps are highly social animals, and Nim's isolation must have exacted a considerable toll. On the other hand there is no question that, while there, Nim is safe.

Thus the upshot of the entire contretemps is that Ally has been stripped of his identity, and Nim is in exile in Texas. Looking back, Chris O'Sullivan, who set all these events in motion with her telephone call to her aunt at CBS, said not long ago that it "would have been better for the chimps in the end had I never made that phone call."

PART FOUR

A Glimmer
of Hope

CHAPTER THIRTEEN

A Glimmer of Hope

WHILE chimps were being shuttled around the United States, I kept hearing reports about Lucy's life in Africa. Although most of these reports stressed the hazards Lucy and Janis faced, and the inappropriateness of trying to educate a suburbanite like Lucy to the wilds, I still felt that perhaps what Janis was doing offered the only glimmer of hope for captive chimps.

And so I went to The Gambia in July 1982 to visit Janis Carter and to see for myself how things were working out. Obviously they had worked out to some degree, because Janis was still there. I cannot say that Janis was initially welcoming about the idea of a visit. She is very proprietary about Lucy and her work, and in the past few years almost no outsiders have been allowed to visit her. While I was there, I did talk to Eddie Brewer, as well as to a few other people acquainted with Janis's work with chimps. And since my return, I have done some checking on the things I was told by various parties, and, not to my surprise, I have discovered that there is no less contradiction and intrigue concerning events in Lucy's life in Africa than there was concerning Washoe's activities in Oklahoma. Still, Janis did not shy away from difficult questions.

Apart from Janis, Eddie Brewer has been the key person in Lucy's life in Africa, and he deserves some introduction. (Stella Brewer divides her time between Africa and the Philippines, where her husband is a forester. She was not in Africa during my visit.) Eddie Brewer has been in The Gambia for well over twenty-six years, first as part of the forestry department and since 1976 as the creator and head of the country's wildlife department. Brewer is not a scientist, and he is not particularly sophisticated about wildlife management, but he does love animals and nature. He is also a good storyteller.

In the early 1970s, Brewer got the idea to try to rehabilitate chimps to the wild as a result of a problem he was having at Abuko Reserve. One of three free-roaming chimps in Abuko Reserve started wreaking havoc with the aid of some captive, orphaned chimps. Brewer would show up at the chimp compound in the morning to find the outside of the place a mess. It looked like the work of chimps, but all the chimps would be safely inside. He was puzzled until one night he secreted himself to observe what happened after the last vehicle had left. The compound was walled on the inside with corrugated iron which Brewer thought was tall enough and slippery enough to be unscalable. What he discovered was that after the last vehicle left, a rehabilitated, wild chimp named Tina would appear out of the bush, climb the wooden outside of the wall, and then, holding on to the top of the wall, she would lower herself enough so that the chimps on the inside could grab her ankles and haul themselves up. The captives would have a grand time of freedom and then return before the first person arrived in the morning. Brewer decided then that there might be a way to get the orphaned chimps out of cages altogether and back into a wild setting.

Brewer is an affable, soft-spoken man, but, according to the testimony of a number of people he has worked with, he can also be quite dominating, even menacing. Janis Carter's relations with him have been uneasy, and for Janis the months in Abuko were a hellish time. Lucy was not making progress, and Janis herself found that her own situation was not on very stable footing. She lived (and lives) in perpetual uncertainty about whether her visa would be renewed, or whether some other event might separate her from Lucy, leaving the chimp miserable, in limbo between civilization and freedom.

During this period in Abuko, Janis lived in an eight-foot-square treehouse in the reserve. She spent a good deal of time learning what she could about which plants and fruits were edible and which were not, and when various plants and trees were in fruit. It was while she was in Abuko that she had an unfortunate run-in with safari ants. Safari ants are a distinctive feature of the African landscape. They march in columns, and woe to any edible thing that happens to be in their path. In this case it was Janis. One night, asleep within the customary protection of mosquito netting, she woke to find that strands of her hair had fallen through the netting and that ants had begun to climb up over her body. She looked around the room to discover that she and her entire room were virtually carpeted with the ants. She knew that safari ants had killed a favorite adult male chimp at Abuko, Buddha, and intimations of her own mortality passed through her mind. She saw little spiders jumping around that were being eaten alive. She ripped off her ant-covered nightclothes and then had to climb down the ladder, also covered with ants. When she tried to brush them out of her hair, the ants bit into her scalp. Her inability to get at them brought her close to the edge of panic, and she ran naked the mile to the Brewers' house, where together they killed the remaining ants with alcohol. It was an experience she remembered five years later with a shudder.

Apart from Janis's traumas, progress in teaching Lucy to adapt was slow to the point of being virtually unnoticeable. Janis could not take Lucy out of her cage, but she could roam around with a young male chimp named Dash. Whenever Dash showed an interest in forage, Janis would bring some of what he was eating back to the cage to try to entice Lucy. She did not have much success, but, she recalls, Lucy did start eating netto pods while at Abuko. Netto pods look like oversized vanilla beans and taste sweet and starchy.

After some time in Abuko, Janis began to think of moving the chimps to the Baboon Islands. She had heard about the islands not too long after arrival in The Gambia, but it was no easy matter to convince Eddie Brewer to let her take Lucy, Marianne, Dash, and some other younger chimps (former captives also awaiting repatriation to the forests) upriver to these islands. Even so, long before she got permission, she began making regular trips up to the islands to get an idea of the vegetation and food supply.

The Baboon Islands, also called the River Gambia National Park, are in fact The Gambia's only national park. Being home to a variety of health-threatening pests, such as the tsetse fly, the islands are not a popular weekend destination. The variety of pests also explains why the islands have been allowed to become a national park—no one really wanted them. In 1978, the only way to get to the islands was either to travel upriver by boat or to drive ten hours along dirt roads in various stages of impassability. As it is, the total area of all The Gambia's parks is less than a quarter of 1 percent of the country's total land area. Today there is a nice asphalt road that covers about three quarters of the 136 miles between Banjul and the Baboon Islands. The islands themselves are remote from any traveled road, and as such offer an incongruous pocket of tranquillity in one of Africa's more densely populated nations.

The Baboon Islands are, in fact, quite rich in wildlife.

Hippos and crocodiles make their home in the brown, blood-warm River Gambia. Goliath herons, sacred ibis, egrets, and other wading birds forage on the mudbanks. On the island, baboons, vervet monkeys, leopards, and hyenas cohabitate in an uneasy, constantly challenged truce, while fish eagles patrol the river from the high branches of its forest cover. Within earshot, on the shores, colobus and patas monkeys enjoy the refuge of this relatively remote place, and occasionally one sees evolutionary oddities such as the giant hornbill walking through the brush. Add to this a magnificent array of poisonous snakes and world-class insects, and you have a nearly complete spectrum of wildlife. Missing are elephants, which vanished from the area fifty years ago; also missing are wild chimps, which used to be common in The Gambia.

The Gambia lies between the Sahel to the north and the rain forests to the south. Its climate might best be described as sub-Sahelian. The Gambia has a good number of trees, but it also must endure a lengthy dry season. The island Janis had in mind, called Baboon Island, is about ten miles long, but its size is deceptive. Because of the extensive swampland, only about 600 out of its 1,200 acres are habitable and productive for chimps. Brewer feels that the substantial baboon population indicates that the island has a high carrying capacity. However, the only real estimates for the amount of forest needed to support chimp populations come from Geza Teleki, a Kenyan primate specialist. He has estimated three chimps per square mile as a maximum density, which would place the ceiling for Baboon Island at about seven chimps, even in the most optimistic scenario.

Janis's troop consisted of nine chimps, which meant that even if she could get her chimps on the island, it was questionable whether the island could support her group without outside food supplements.

After attempting all manner of argument and persuasion, Janis finally obtained Eddie Brewer's consent to allow her to move her chimps to Baboon Island. Her relationship with Eddie Brewer over the years has been not measurably less contentious than her relationship with Lemmon back in the United States. Janis was in an awkward situation in The Gambia in that she likes to have her own way and to run her own show, and yet she found herself quite dependent, not just on Brewer's good humor but also on his active support. She was on the Brewers'—Eddie and Stella's—turf. She could raise some of the funds she needed to keep going herself, but no matter how much money she raised, she could never be institutionally independent of Eddie Brewer. This has made for some rousing arguments over the years, since Eddie Brewer and Janis Carter do not have the same philosophy of wildlife management, and it has also aggravated Janis's insecurity about Lucy and her future in Africa.

In this context, the move to the island was a significant coup. It got Janis and Eddie out of each other's way, but more important, it put Janis and her chimps in a setting that was much closer to what Janis had envisioned when she left the States for Africa. On Baboon Island there was the possibility that Lucy might pull herself together.

Things did indeed begin to improve for both Lucy and Janis when they moved to the Baboon Islands in May 1979. At first Janis had Baboon Island to herself and the chimps she brought there with her. The group consisted of Lucy, Marianne, and seven African-born chimps. Janis gave them all names. The writer Lillian Hellman probably died without knowing that her writing inspired two of the names Janis gave to her chimps. Dash, now ten, had been captured in the wild in Guinea at about age four. He was so named because Janis was taken with Lillian Hellman's nickname for Dashiell Hammett. Hellman's memoirs were also the source for the name Lily, which Janis gave to another chimp in the group. Lily had been caught in Zaire for the pet trade when she was two and a half. She had been in poor shape when she was caught and was nursed back to health by an American couple before being turned over to the Brewers. Lily was an inveterate and unrepentant prankster.

Another chimp was named Lakey after a character in Mary McCarthy's novel *The Group*, though Janis said that the name, which she gave to a female chimp from Guinea, was not a statement about the chimp's sexual preference (in the novel, Lakey was a lesbian). The other names had more prosaic origins.

Karen had had the most experience in the wild prior to an interlude in captivity. Janis would learn wild chimp behaviors by watching Karen and then pass on the lessons to the other chimps where necessary. Then there was Kit, a female who was blind in one eye, Geza, a young male named for Geza Teleki whom Lucy adopted as a son, and Marti, a not very intimidating male. The last four chimps all came from Sierra Leone and had been destined for Europe before being confiscated en route to Holland. These four were the last in Janis's band to be moved to the Baboon Islands.

It was far from being a characteristic group of chimps. Dash, the oldest male, was only five when they moved to the island. The dominant figure was Janis, and the dominant chimp was Lucy, a female. She would not have been the dominant chimp if there had been an adult male around, or even a strange adult female, but the only other large chimp in the group was Marianne, who was several years Lucy's junior. Lucy certainly did not dominate by reason of her knowledge of life in the bush. During the first year on Baboon Island, she would surely have been glad to exchange her new life for a motel room.

For the first two years, Janis and her chimps had the island to themselves, but then Stella Brewer's chimps in

Senegal came under attack by neighboring wild chimp bands. When an adult female was killed, the Brewers decided to move their chimps onto the islands as well. Janis fought this idea for two years, but having been out of the country for a time, she returned to find that Stella Brewer had moved thirteen chimps onto the other end of the island.

There are five Baboon Islands, of which three are suitable as homes for chimps. When I arrived in Africa, there were thirty-two chimps scattered throughout the three islands. Janis and her troop of nine chimps still shared Baboon Island with thirteen of Stella's chimps. The two bands are separated by a marshy area which makes an ineffective barrier because it dries up during the dry season.

Janis's home on the island was a cage built by some obliging commandos from the British armed forces who were on bush maneuvers nearby when Janis first moved to Baboon Island. And so she lived in the cage while the chimps slept outdoors. The evidence is that at first the chimps would have loved to reverse this situation. They would sleep on top of her cage, and when they were frightened, which was not infrequently, they would relieve themselves upon Janis. She quickly took care to get something to protect her from the various elements, and she also took steps to encourage the chimps to sleep elsewhere.

On the mainland, five miles downriver from Janis's cage, the Brewers established a small encampment from which they tended their chimp colonies. When I visited Baboon Island, I stayed down in this camp, and Janis and I would steer her little skiff up to her cage in the mornings.

At first, I was more impressed by the island's beauty than by any of the hazards the island or river presented. In the mornings, the jungle would erupt with sounds as its extraordinarily rich and contentious population came to life. But I could also see how the place might pose a challenge to someone who had to spend many months there alone. Carol Ball, a personable and candid young woman from England, who worked with Stella Brewer's chimps, was preparing to leave when I visited the islands. She said that both the loneliness and the hazards of the area had made her progressively more frightened as the months went by. She had worked in an animal park in England before coming to The Gambia, so she was not unused to animals. However, she had had a couple of frightening run-ins with some of Stella's chimps during food drops from a boat, and she found herself beginning to dread forays into the bush or upriver. She spoke admiringly of Stella's fearlessness in plunging through the brush and noted wistfully that she had come to the conclusion that she would never be her match in that respect.

A story like Carol's puts Janis's remarkable adaptation into perspective. Janis certainly is not fearless—indeed, she spoke frequently about her fears. But she made the adjustment to this lonely life, and she clearly acquired a good deal of knowledge of the forests. In Abuko she slept in a treehouse, and she was not more than a mile from help at any time. In the Baboon Islands, Janis quite often slept outside with the chimps, and there was no human being she could turn to for help. As we shall see, she found that in an emergency she could turn to Lucy for help.

I spoke to Janis both in the camp and in her cage while Dash made halfhearted attempts on my life through the bars. During our conversations, a thin, dignified-looking chimp appeared from the forest and hovered in the leaves not far from the cage. This was Lucy. I was the first person from Lucy's old life who had visited Janis in Africa. Lucy stared and stared at this figure, which seemed to stir some faint sense of recognition in the depths of her memory. But apart from her interest in our conversation, Lucy fit so well into her surroundings that she might have been one of The Gambia's vanished native chimps. While Lucy observed, Janis told me about their long journey to the wilds.

CHAPTER FOURTEEN

Lucy on
Baboon Island

THE MOST dramatic moments of my visits to Janis's cage were the arrivals and exits. Before taking the boat upriver to her little jetty on the island, Janis would pile stacks of netto pods in the front of the boat. Then, as we approached the jetty, she would pull the boat in toward a tree stuck out over the water fifty feet downstream from the jetty. I would take over maneuvering the boat, and Janis would move to the bow. Meanwhile the chimps, who recognized the sound of Janis's outboard, mysteriously appeared on the riverbank to greet her and to size me up. The netto pods served as a distraction to allow Janis to hustle me inside her cage before the chimps decided to do something I might regret. They regard Janis as a member of their group, and had they perceived me as a threat to Janis, she claims that they would have had no hesitancy in attacking me.

The first morning, I slowly edged the boat in enough so that Janis could toss the netto pods onto the shore. Janis had been away from the island for a week, so she hopped ashore and spent some time greeting her co-pains. This was cause for great excitement, and the chimps screamed and then turned to sorting the spoils according to their dominance hierarchy. Janis then hopped back in the boat, and I drove the boat over to the jetty. Janis quickly got me inside the cage, a moment before Dash, who seemed to have sized me up as fit for a coffin, came rocketing toward the cage, netto leaf in one hand, with intimidation plainly on his mind.

The cage has something of the flavor of a Robinson Crusoe setting. Amid the paraphernalia of camping are incongruous reminders of civilization, such as a type-writer and files. Much of the space inside the cage is taken up by a large tent whose front flaps create a ve-randa of sorts. On top of the cage is a pile of branches. At the time of my visit, in July 1982, the cage had been Janis's home for a little more than three years. During that time, she had left the island on numerous occasions, including one period in the United States that kept her away for several weeks; the great majority of her time had been spent exploring the island with her chimp fam-ily.

Our conversations focused on Lucy. Apart from Janis's attachment to Lucy, she was also the most diffi-cult chimp by far to teach the basics of being a normal, wild chimp. All the others (with the exception of Mar-ianne, who was much younger) had benefited from some wild rearing, and the adjustments, while difficult, were not as radical as they were for Lucy. Lucy's history on Baboon Island broke down into two distinct periods: the first year, which was a period of frustration and at times near despair for Janis, and the period from the end of the first year to the present. The beginning of the second period was marked by a watershed event, from which point onward Lucy made steady progress.

Although she had the cage, at first Janis spent a good deal of time sleeping outside with the chimps. She wanted to teach them quickly about living in trees. This is where chimps ordinarily sleep, and it is also a lot safer for them than sleeping on the ground.

She built a platform in a nearby tree and would bend branches and leaves into a nest. The platform served as a halfway house in getting Lucy and Marianne off the ground. Before too long, Lucy began to sleep in trees, but she would sleep in the fork of sturdy branches rather than out among the leaves, like the other chimps. So far as I know, Janis has been unable to get the earthbound Lucy to move beyond her safe but uncomfortable fork-hostels. Although the other chimps have learned to build nests out among the leaves, unlike wild chimps they will use a nest more than once, a practice that quickly leads to some squalid accommodations.

Some of the differences between Janis's troop and wild chimps can be explained by the fact that Janis's chimps are confined to an island that limits the nomadic wanderings that are typical of chimps; some also have to do with the difficulty of trying to create a chimp society from scratch. Janis could not force the chimps to move each night for sanitary reasons. Moreover, since she has had to teach them by example, she would have had to risk her own neck in attempting to build a new nest in a high place every day. It was a risk she could not afford to take, for if she had fallen and broken a bone or two, she would have had only the chimps to provide her with the necessary first aid.

Teaching by example meant eating all the foods the chimps ate or should eat and hoping that they would emulate her. When she saw an edible leaf, Janis would imitate chimp food barks and point the way. If the leaves were in a tree, Janis would climb to a low branch and enthusiastically munch on the leaves, making satisfied grunts to let the chimps know that they were missing out on a real treat. The more suspicious chimps would settle about an inch from Janis's face and minutely scrutinize her eating. Sometimes a chimp would open Janis's mouth to inspect the partially chewed food.

While Lucy eventually began to eat wild foods that Janis gathered for her, she resisted gathering food herself. Janis recalls, "Anything that I thought Lucy would benefit from I would do." This meant using sign language and spoken language, as well as example. Janis did this because of the urgency she felt about Lucy's failure to adapt.

The fact that Lucy and Janis had a special bond actually enhanced Lucy's status as the dominant chimp since Janis was the supreme being in the Baboon Island universe. "If Lucy were among chimps her own size," says Janis, "she would be at the bottom in rank." However, because Lucy was the oldest and largest, the younger chimps automatically looked to her and to Marianne when they first arrived. Janis notes that Marianne "was dumb as could be and knew absolutely nothing and would go out in the swamp and do incredibly stupid things, but even Karen, as wild as she was, would follow Marianne around because she was bigger." This went on until Karen got more familiar with her surroundings, and then, Janis notes, "it became obvious that Karen knew what she was doing, and Marianne would follow her lead."

For the first year, Lucy clung to her relationship with Janis. She would not groom other chimps and she would not drink from the river. "Lucy saw me drinking from a bottle," says Janis, "and that's what she wanted to do." In essence there were two groups—Janis and Lucy, and Janis and the rest of the chimps. It turned out that there were a number of things which Lucy found it difficult to master. The other chimps had a tremendous advantage in having learned to climb and live in trees during their infancy. Until she reached Baboon Island, Lucy had only limited climbing experience, and the cornucopia of the forest canopy was at first almost as inaccessible to her as it was to Janis. Janis would do things such as tying bunches of fruits to low branches in order to encourage Lucy to forage for herself.

Janis also had to overcome a number of aversions in order to serve as a proper role model for the chimps. "I learned from the wilder chimps," she said, and then she would teach the more middle-class chimps. For instance, she learned about eating safari ants from Dash. Wild chimps gather safari ants on the end of a stick and then eat them. It was something Janis thought the other chimps would have to learn how to do:

"I was scared about eating ants. . . . I probably never would have tried it if Dash hadn't done it first." Janis was prompted to act because she could see that Lily was not learning to eat the ants even though she had Dash's example to follow. Her policy was not to intervene unless she thought it necessary, and so she waited until it became obvious that Lily was not going to do it unless Janis did it first. She began by practicing eating the ants without the chimps around. "Then one day it was like, Today has got to be the day you do it. . . . I was careful enough to make sure I only had a few ants on the end of a stick, and then I was careful to make sure I placed the stick in my teeth and not in my jaw so that I would be able to smash 'em immediately." Lily was sufficiently impressed to begin eating the ants herself. Lucy was not impressed then with the idea of eating safari ants, and she is not impressed now with the idea of eating safari ants.

Lucy's first big breakthrough in terms of gathering food for herself had to do with eating the leaves and flowers of the baobab tree. Baobab, which is relatively abundant on the island, is a rich source of food for the chimps. They eat the leaves, flowers, bark, and fruit. Lucy took a liking to the leaves and flowers, but she was still unwilling to gather them herself, and the large trunks of the trees posed a daunting obstacle in terms of climbing. In an article Janis wrote for *Smithsonian* magazine, she describes how she got Lucy to deal with this obstacle:

...she had difficulty [climbing]... the thick-trunked baobab. So she would sit under the tree and wait for the cast-off food of the other chimps. She grew to like the leaves and flowers so much that when she watched the others from below, she began signing to me to help her. She signed, "More food, you go," pointing to the others who were devouring the tasty food.

I am not an adept climber myself; moreover, it was Lucy who had to learn actively to gather her food, not me. I communicated "No," and showed her an alternate route up a neighboring tree, from which she could then leap across to the baobab. This did not appeal to her and she persisted in her efforts to get me to help her. She led me by the hand to the tree base and placed my hands on the trunk as she repeated, "More food, Jan go." As a final attempt to assist her without actually gathering her food, I returned to camp with her close on my heels. There I had a large piece of construction timber, which I started dragging back to the baobab tree site. Lucy seemed to anticipate my action and helped me take the timber to the tree, where she immediately propped it up against the trunk, giving her access to the food.

The great breakthrough was when Lucy first cracked open a baobab fruit. Janis described this to me as we sat in her cage: "She would always hand it [the baobab fruit] to me to open. She has got the strength to do it, she just wants to be pampered. I would say "No, you have to do it yourself," and finally she did it. It was as if everybody else knew it was her first time, because they all stopped what they were doing and were watching her. It was a really big deal when she first cracked open the baobab. Probably in time she would have picked up those food habits without my being here, but I don't think that she would have made it to this stage without me."

Despite small victories, progress was slow, and Janis remembers that even after a year on the island, she was still thinking that perhaps she had made a mistake in bringing Lucy there, and that all her efforts might have been for naught. At the time, Janis was severely stretched financially, and she felt stretched in every other way as well. At this low point, the chimps did something that infuriated Janis but that turned out to be a turning point in Lucy's adaptation to the wild and to her chimp peers.

What they did was to tear down the back of Janis's cage. "This may sound sick," Janis recalls, "but I was so mad at the ungratefulness, I remember thinking, Fuck them, they're not going to have any more food; they can either make it or not make it. I just cut off the food.

"Lucy got pathetically thin. And Lucy would just sit there and sign all the time: 'Food . . . drink . . . Jan come out . . . Lucy's hurt.' She would find a 'hurt' and say, 'Hurt.' She would whine and start pulling her hair out. It was so hard to ignore it, and what I finally had to do was to stop her from having visual contact with me. I made her go back and sit behind the cage. I'd say, 'I don't want to see you.' So she would go back around the corner there, back where she could barely, barely see me. Then she would slowly move up until she was in view. This went on for six days. And finally I decided I had to go out and help her be miserable, and so I would go out with the group, and she still wouldn't go away from the cage. It got to the point where I thought she might not have the physical strength to go, and I started going shorter distances.

"Then one day she just broke. I was at my absolute wits' end. I didn't think she was going to eat a leaf. I didn't think she was going to do anything, and we had fight after fight after fight. We fell asleep on the ground next to each other—we weren't having contact with each other—and when I woke up, it was as though she had decided during her nap that she was going to start trying. She sat up and picked a leaf within arm's reach and handed it to me to eat it, and I ate it and then shared it with her. After that she started trying. I don't know how much longer she could have gone on, or myself, either. I was to my absolute limit."

Janis describes her role as that of a psychologist who has to break down barriers before behavior can change. Her total repudiation of Lucy succeeded where her earlier cajolings had failed. From this point onward, Lucy made steady progress, learning from Janis as well as from the wilder chimps.

For her part Janis discovered that Lucy was a true friend. On one occasion Dash playfully grabbed Janis's hair. Perhaps frightened by his own boldness Dash got excited and began to tighten his grip. Seeing that Janis was in trouble, Lucy rushed up, grabbed Dash with her teeth, and threw him aside.

One casualty of the three-month-long traumatic period was sign language. Janis still uses English with Lucy and with the other chimps. (While we were talking, Lily attempted to heist the boat, which prompted Janis to scream at her to get out of the boat.) Janis also uses a lot of chimp language to communicate with the group. But she decided that using sign language set up a special bond between Lucy and her that excluded others. Moreover, she does not think sign language has anything to do with being a chimp. Nor does she think that the language has enhanced our understanding of chimps. She named one prominent sign-language experimenter and proponent, and said, "He's worked with sign language and chimps for years, and I don't think he knows anything about what chimps are like." Later she said, "I stopped signing at the point when . . . the next thing that I had to teach [Lucy] was that she had to be part of a social group with other chimps. The sign language was just too strong a tie. . . . I'm not going to be with Lucy forever, and I would like to see visually that I have prepared her for my not being here." In fact, Janis sees little value in sign-language studies at all.

Ironically, although Janis has stopped signing, Lucy has not. Janis reports that she still uses more than twenty signs when around Janis. It must be confusing for Lucy to find that Ameslan, which everybody made such a fuss about when she was young, has now become a faux pas.

All the while we talked, Lucy stationed herself on the remains of the platform Janis had built for her and stared and stared. She would not approach the cage—something she ordinarily did on the rare occasions when Janis brought a visitor to the island—nor did she move off to join the others. I desperately wanted to sign to her, but one of the ground rules of my visit was that Lucy was to be signed to only after she initiated signing herself. And so I had no means of renewing our acquaintance.

CHAPTER FIFTEEN

In the Shadow of Man

JANIS can be quite obstinate, but she also possesses the curiosity of the born scientist. She was intrigued by Lucy's reaction to seeing me; being as eager as I was to know what Lucy made of my visit, she decided that for one day she could relax the prohibition against signing. Lucy was still obediently stationed outside the cage, and Janis signed to her, "Who he?" At first Lucy couldn't believe that Janis was signing again, and so Janis had to repeat "Who he?" several times. It had been well over a year since Janis had stopped signing with Lucy. Finally Lucy responded.

At first she signed, "Roger," a sign made by grabbing the ear lobe between thumb and forefinger, but then, and much more persistently, she kept signing, "Lucy Janis ...Lucy Janis, Lucy Janis." It appeared that Lucy did associate me with her old life in America. Lucy may have thought that I was there to take her back to America, or to replace Janis, or to come between Janis and her in some way. My feeling was that the bond between

Janis and Lucy was still very strong, whether it was expressed through sign language or not.

I left the island somewhat frustrated. I thought that the question of how Lucy would use sign language to deal with the stresses of her new life was worth exploring. Similarly I wondered about whether Lucy had attempted to use the language to communicate with the other chimps, and whether they had picked up signs from her. In response to these and other questions about sign language, Janis was vague and largely noncommittal, promising to write me in the future once she had had a chance to go through her notes. She never did. Janis is just not interested in sign language—she says, "It has nothing to do with being a wild chimp"—and for Janis that is the end of it.

After I left The Gambia, Lucy and the other chimps made it clear that they took very seriously any real or imagined threat to separate them from Janis. When I saw Janis in the United States some months after my visit, Janis told me that for a long time after my departure, the chimps would not let anyone else come on the island and that they made it almost impossible for Janis to leave.

The years that Janis and Lucy have spent together have created a bond that makes it as hard for Janis to let go of Lucy as it is for Lucy to let go of Janis. "It's a little like seeing your daughter go off to college," she says. She also has strong bonds with the other chimps—particularly Dash, the young male that almost did her in.

She is somewhat apprehensive about the moment when she will have to break her ties to the chimps. This moment may come when it is no longer safe for her to go onto the island. Even now Dash has begun to challenge Janis's dominance, and she has nothing beyond bluff with which to respond. I think that, unless threats to her own safety make it necessary, Janis will not voluntarily break with her chimp band.

Apart from the question of whether or not Baboon Island can support her chimp band, a number of prob-

lems and potential threats make Baboon Island at best a
temporary refuge for the chimps. Janis and Eddie
Brewer have had an uneasy relationship over the years.
They appear to have fundamentally different ideas about
what type of program might best serve the needs of the
chimpanzees. Brewer is not unduly worried if the former
captives are not totally independent from food drops.
Janis, on the other hand, is perhaps unrealistic in her
search for the perfect refuge. Still, if Janis were more
realistic, she probably would have given up long ago.

With good reason, Janis is unwilling to leave the
chimps to their fate. At the same time, she agrees that
true freedom for Lucy and the other eight chimps will
come only when neither Janis nor any other human
beings really know where they are. The problem right
now is that not only does Janis know where the chimps
are, but a lot of other people do too. The chimps' future
is threatened by pressures to use Baboon Island for various purposes which range from the commercial exploi-
tation of the project by bringing tour boats to the island
to view the chimps, to the use of the island for mosquito
research. Members of The Gambian government used to
remind Janis of these possibilities periodically, and after
listening to one such conversation, I got the impression
that part of the purpose was to keep Janis in perpetual
insecurity about her future in The Gambia. There is also
the very real threat that a dam will be built on the Gambia River, and the dam might spell the end of Baboon
Island itself. Finally the Brewers keep putting more and
more chimps on the island, which guarantees that the
chimps will need food drops, and which raises the
spectre of conflicts between the chimp bands.

Janis takes these threats to heart. If any were realized, it would nullify the efforts of the last eight years of
her life. She hates the idea that she might have spent her
youth in The Gambia only to see the chimps end up in an
African, rather than an American, zoo.

Although Lucy and the other chimps live a more wild

life than any captive chimp, the fragility of their freedom is underscored by the image of Janis roaming through Africa looking for a refuge for the nine chimps that will not be in the shadow of man. The sad probability is that these and other chimps—even those now wild—will always be a hostage to the whims of man.

A year after my visit, Lucy became very ill. I had put Janis in touch with Jim Mahoney of LEMSIP, and he flew over to examine Lucy and the other chimps. His secondary purpose was to see whether Janis's approach was a viable alternative to the grim destiny facing chimps in laboratories in the United States.

When Mahoney saw her, Lucy was extremely thin and weak. He diagnosed the illness as chronic anemia, possibly brought on by hookworm. Because the chimps are on a fairly small island, they tend to follow regular paths through the bush, and this increases the likelihood of hookworm. Without treatment, Mahoney feels that Lucy would have been dead in a matter of weeks. The treatment consisted of three transfusions and a diet supplement.

During the six days Lucy spent in captivity, Mahoney says that she began to revert to her former dependent state. Mahoney also says that the health crisis threw Janis into a profound depression about whether Lucy and the other chimps might ever be free.

Her anxieties were aggravated by the fact that plans to dam the Gambia River had proceeded during the year. The idea behind the dam is that it would form a barrier, preventing salinity from the ocean from moving as far upriver as it now does, and thus the dam would increase the acreage available for rice production. In a country as densely populated and as poor as The Gambia, it is hard to argue the case of nonnative chimps over native Gambians, particularly when there is Kuwaiti money immediately available to build the dam.

Jim Mahoney came back from his trip impressed with the effort Janis has put into habituating her charges to the wild but daunted by the prospect of doing what she has done for more than an extremely limited number of chimps. He does feel, however, that what Janis is doing could be done on a larger scale if people took care to find the right animals to rehabilitate—wild-born chimps, for example, instead of captive-born. But he cautions that some labs would use the notion of rehabilitation as a cover for dumping unprepared and perhaps even disease-contaminated chimps into the wild in order to escape the financial responsibility of caring for the animals. There are already charges that this has happened elsewhere in Africa.

Jim Mahoney does not feel that Lucy was a proper candidate for rehabilitation because of her extreme identification with people. On the other hand, whatever her future, Lucy has for a few years lived the life of a chimp in the wild—something only she and Marianne out of 1,700 captive chimps in America have had a chance to do.

Still, Lucy has lived at the sufferance of the people around her. Having been initiated into the mysteries of language, she then found herself required by her human guardians to return to the condition of a wild chimp. She found herself stripped of her privileges and discouraged from using the system of communication that she had spent the better part of her youth learning. At different times in her life, human beings have been parents, mentors, friends, jailors, rulers, judges, owners, and gods. She now waits, perhaps wondering what she really is, and what our bizarre, moody species has in store for her next.

PART FIVE

Poor Relations

CHAPTER SIXTEEN

The Bottom Line

PERHAPS the final irony of the tempest surrounding the sale of language-using chimps to a medical laboratory is that the situation facing chimps today is far more perilous than it was two years ago. Recently the Centers for Disease Control in Atlanta, Georgia, announced that chimps had been successfully infected with the dread disease AIDS as part of an effort to study the disease and perhaps develop a vaccine. None of the chimps in the AIDS work were known to the outside world, and consequently the news passed without inspiring the protests that greeted the sale of Ally and Nim to LEMSIP. Nevertheless, this news signals ominous new changes in the climate that conditions the use of captive apes.

Which brings us back to Jim Mahoney. Mahoney was cast as a villain in 1982, but today, long after the public has forgotten Ally and Nim, he continues to lobby in his "wicked" way to protect laboratory primates. Mahoney is an interesting man, and it is worth considering his perspective on the situation of chimps, which does not easily fall into one category or another. Mahoney's title at LEMSIP is Director of Primate Reproduction, but in reality he functions as the person in charge of the primate colony. He was born and raised in Ireland and came to this country about thirteen years ago.

Notwithstanding the fact that he works for a laboratory that uses primates in medical experimentation, he is truly dedicated to animals of all species. When I first met him, he was devoting his lunch hours to playing with a couple of small rhesus monkeys who had been orphaned. He has taken a great deal of trouble to try to understand the ways in which chimps and other primates communicate among themselves, and, as noted earlier, he prefers to communicate with them in what he understands to be their own language rather than through sign language.

If Mahoney clearly has sentimental feelings for his chimp charges, he is quite unsentimental in addressing the forces that threaten their future. He has worked since 1980 as a member of The Chimpanzee Task Force of the Interagency Research Animal Committee, a National Institutes of Health task force bent upon devising some coherent policy to govern the administration of chimp research in the United States. Although Mahoney's concern is for the chimps, the task force's mandate is to devise a way to ensure a continued supply of chimps for research purposes. The task force consists of about thirty scientists and research-facility officials drawn from institutions around the country. Given the committee's composition, Mahoney has been in a good position to monitor the mood of those people who decide the destiny of the apes, and the signs have grown more disquieting as the years pass. The reality Mahoney witnesses at meetings of the task force is one in which chimps are not a higher animal entitled to special status but a commodity whose value diminishes rapidly once the animal has been used for research.

Mahoney says that never once has he heard it brought up during meetings of the task force that chimps are entitled to special treatment because of their standing in the natural order. On the contrary, the big issue facing the research community is the question of euthanasia, and by Mahoney's estimate, more than half the task force in 1984 was in favor of euthanasia as a way of dealing with the growing burden of adult male chimps that have already been used in research or testing and are unsuitable for breeding. In fact, Mahoney is convinced that somewhere in the country euthanasia has already been used as a way of reducing the "surplus" (as it is described) chimp population. "Once you stop to think, you know that money is the determining factor [affecting the chimps' future]," says Mahoney, "and once you know that money is the determining factor, you know what is going to happen."

Even if a research facility does not fall back on euthanasia, the pressure of an ever-growing surplus chimp population acts as an added incentive to use these chimps in terminal studies. This pressure is one element of the mix of forces which has made chimps tempting subjects for AIDS research. Says Mahoney, "AIDS must have been a blessing because it gave them [the primate facilities] a good reason to use the animals in a terminal study. It's a matter of simple arithmetic."

Given the panicked search for a solution that this fearsome disease has inspired, it is unlikely that the issue will be addressed rationally. The victims and potential victims want to know the cause and the cure of AIDS—fast—and the question of whether the chimps' higher status should exempt them from such research understandably tends to get lost in such circumstances. Nor, as Mahoney points out, do the chimps find an ally in their keepers, who, likely as not, have been looking for a "use" for the animals. The result is that while the decision to send sign-language-using chimps to a medical lab for serum testing produced initial howls of protest, the news in August 1984 that laboratory chimps had been successfully infected with AIDS was announced without incident. In fact, a news account of this "breakthrough" written by Lawrence Altman in the *New York Times* at no point mentioned that this use of chimpanzees might be thought to be controversial.

As someone who both loves chimpanzees and recognizes the realities of the economics that govern their use in captivity, Mahoney has devised what he considers to be a viable plan to serve the interests of the captive chimp "community" in the United States. To start with, Mahoney does not see a back-to-Africa movement as an alternative for captive American chimps. After all, Janis Carter has devoted eight years of her life to securing the future of Lucy and her small band, and even now their future is not certain. Mahoney also feels that the idea of rehabilitation to the wild is prone to abuse by labs who, operating under cover of the noblest ideals, will use the idea as an excuse to dump chimps back into nature without the preparation that might give them a fair shot at survival. Or, perhaps worse, a lab might put into the wild chimps that pose an epidemiological hazard to neighboring wild chimpanzees.

Thus Mahoney feels that the problem of what kind of future captive chimps will have must be solved in the United States. His task force proposed a plan by which a large breeding colony of about 650 chimps would be protected and federally maintained in enlightened circumstances (which means extended family groupings) in perpetuity. Ten percent of this colony would be "harvested" each year for research. Since the bulk of research needs would involve young chimps, this "harvest" would work out to about 50 percent of the newborn chimps, something which Mahoney readily acknowledges is not a happy prospect. Still, he feels that such a trade-off is the only realistic way to improve the lot of chimps. If nothing else, Mahoney feels that lab owners would be forced to upgrade their facilities and standards to qualify for federal money.

The fate of one part of this proposal reveals the bizarre logic that determines the welfare of chimps in America. One part of Mahoney's proposal called for money to be budgeted to maintain the present population of "spent" research animals for at least two years after their use in research. This proposal was dropped, one source told me, because the group decided that to approach Congress on the issue of raising money for two years would raise question in congressional minds about what would happen to the animals after the budgeted period. If this is the case, then we might assume that those charged with governing the use of chimpanzees in research are literally burying the issue. If true, the reasoning behind the decision also contains a less than complimentary estimation of the intelligence and inquisitiveness of members of Congress.

There is no guarantee that Congress will approve any part of the overall proposal, and without question there are many animal rights groups who would find it abhorrent. What is arresting about it is that a thoughtful advocate of chimp welfare such as Mahoney should see no practical alternative to an arrangement that justifies the lives of chimpanzees in terms of their usefulness in solving human medical problems.

Where Mahoney differs with most of the task force is on the question of what to do with those chimps who do not fall within the confines of the task force's recommendation. As noted, Mahoney would have established a type of retirement colony to maintain these chimps and on occasion make them available for various types of research. His colleagues would rather destroy them and so be rid of the problem.

SOMETHING has happened since Mahoney first laid out his arguments—something that demonstrates how the prediction of euthanasia for chimps might eventually become a self-fulfilling prophecy. The event was the publication of a short report in the magazine *Science* that purports to spell out some of the details of the NIH task force's plan. According to the report, the final plan "calls for destroying some of the older animals that either cannot breed or that have been exposed to non-A non-B hepatitis."

Mahoney says that the report on the plan is inaccurate: that there is nothing in the plan that calls for euthanizing chimps. However, he says that it is quite likely that different labs will seize on the report in *Science* as justification for euthanasia, and once that happens, other labs will follow the de facto precedent.

According to Mahoney, euthanasia first arose as a potential solution to the problem of unwanted chimps two years ago during an early meeting of the task force. At that time, two separate groups brought up the idea as a strong possibility. Mahoney says that he was shocked to hear the head of a primate center say that he was in favor of euthanasia, but that before being killed, the animals should be used in a study, "even a trivial study." Mahoney says he replied that "there is no room in science for 'trivial studies.'" No vote was taken regarding this recommendation, and the group decided the issue needed further study. However, in May 1984, at a meeting at Holloman Air Force Base to discuss the task force report, Thomas Wolfle, an NIH veterinarian, referred back to the earlier meeting and remarked, according to Mahoney, "We all agree that euthanasia is an acceptable solution" (regarding the problem of unwanted chimps). At this point, Mahoney says, he pointed out that no one had ever voted on that proposition, nor was there any further study of the matter. He also said that he asserted that euthanasia was a completely unacceptable solution. Mahoney recalls that of the more than thirty people in the room, including noted chimp advocates such as Jo and Paul Fritz of the Primate Foundation of Arizona, only one man, a veterinarian from the South West Foundation, backed him. The silence all but sealed the fate of unwanted chimps.

On the way back from this meeting, Mahoney wrote a letter to officials at NIH in which he made his arguments against euthanasia and for his proposed retirement colony. "I offered several scientific arguments," he notes, "and then followed with ethical arguments. In retrospect that was a mistake. The ethical arguments probably hurt rather than helped my case."

Mahoney has seen how euthanasia might creep in as a solution by observing the process in his own lab. Two unwanted older chimps were shipped off to another research facility to be used in a terminal study. Mahoney says that the chimps were then euthanized to "harvest" tissue samples for the study. But he says that he was told that were it not for the fact that the chimps were going to be killed, the investigator would not have done this study. What tipped the balance was that the chimps were old—nonbreeders.

IN THE early 1970s, when I was researching *Apes, Men, and Language*, anthropologist Harvey Sarles spoke about how our understanding of other animals had been traditionally governed by a cure-orientation in science. He meant by this that we tended to look at other creatures only in terms of how they might help us to understand human nature and cure human problems. Sarles said back then that ethology, the study of the biology of behavior, was one science founded on premises that encouraged researchers to understand animal behavior in the animal's native environment without that cure-orientation. Since the early 1970s, ethology has prospered, and for a while it looked as though science was beginning to study the other creatures in the world apart from questions of humanity's immediate self-interest. But so far, none of this new understanding of the

complexity of the social organization and communication
of animals, particularly apes, has translated into better
treatment in captivity. The situation for the captive
chimp is indeed more perilous today than it was two
years ago, and it was more perilous two years ago than it
was ten years ago.

Ultimately the cause célèbre surrounding the shipment of the sign-language-using chimps led to the re-
moval of one of that number, Nim, to a dubious
retirement in Texas, and another, Ally, to disappear into
a chimp Gulag. It did not affect the treatment of the
other chimps either at LEMSIP or elsewhere. On the
other hand, there is no question that had the subjects of
the AIDS experiments been sign-language-using chimps,
the news would have precipitated a tremendous outcry.
We might well imagine that such news would have led to
rescue attempts similar to those which greeted the news
of serum testing in 1981.

The basic difference between the language-taught
chimp and any other chimp is simply a matter of education. The fact that chimps can use human words and express thoughts and feelings merely gives us a way to
identify with their suffering. We know them, or at least
we know them better than we do the mute, benighted
lumpen proletariat that were used in the AIDS studies.
In truth, unless one offers the argument that their education makes it a waste to use the animals in straight medical research, there is no reason to spare the sign-using
chimp in favor of any other.

Taking these three circumstances together—the outrage over the fate of the language-using chimps, the tran-
sience of that outrage, and the indifference to the fate of
ordinary chimps—we might well conclude that the fate
of the captive chimpanzee has been determined by the
way we have chosen to look at them on any particular
day. And on most days, humanity has acknowledged
evolution to a degree that makes the chimp a surrogate

when things grow difficult for us, but rarely have we acknowledged chimps as brethren. They are indeed poor relations, whose moments of being in favor with their powerful, moody relatives are few and far between.

CHAPTER SEVENTEEN

A Mercurial Relationship

LOOKING back over the saga of his peers in language research, the dispassionate chimp analyst would undoubtedly arrive at the conclusion that when it comes to security, the best relationship to have had with a human is a strong personal one. Ally, who was a good student, ended up stripped of his identity because he had no human sponsor willing to go to the lengths that Penny Patterson, Roger Fouts, or Janis Carter did to secure the future of their pupils. Poor little Nim discovered that fame alone offers dubious guarantees if the human being in your life decides you don't really have what it takes and moves on to other interests. Koko, Washoe, and Lucy, on the other hand, have discovered that there is nothing like a surrogate parent when the mood of the scientific community turns against you.

However, the chimp analyst would be wrong. The chimp, having a slightly smaller brain than his human counterpart, might miss some pieces of the picture, and were the chimp analyst to take these factors into ac-

count, they might lead him to an entirely different conclusion. For instance, given the benefits that have inured
to apes in the hundred years since they were first proposed as our relatives, it would be understandable if the
chimp analyst, looking at the big picture, were to conclude that Darwin was the ape's public enemy number
one, and that it would have been better for the ape family had Wilberforce and Disraeli carried the day when
they weighed in with their opinions on the question of
human ancestry.

Nor is the picture simple from the human point of
view. Although there is no doubt that underlying the actions of Roger Fouts, Penny Patterson, and Janis Carter
is a genuine need to preserve a cherished relationship,
this concern alone is inadequate to account for all their
actions. At different times each of the animals with
whom they have been associated has played a role in the
intellectual and economic life of its protector, as well as
in his or her personal life, and the former roles might
have caused Penny, Roger, and Janis to act in ways that
were not necessarily in the best interests of the ape.

Beyond the question of the ways in which the ten-
sions between these various roles and relationships have
affected the chimps' lives, or the humans' lives, there is
also the question of how each role has affected the other
roles. At different times, critics have charged that the
role of the ape in the sponsor's personal life has affected
its role in his or her scientific life, or that the role of the
chimp in the sponsor's economic life has affected its role
in his or her scientific life.

In fact, one can look at Herb Terrace's charge that
Nim's signing is nothing more than reward-motivated imitation as an assertion that the economic role of the
human in Nim's life conditioned both his intellectual and
personal relationships with his sponsors. But that is getting back to the chimp point of view, and when you consider the chimp's perspective, the permutations of the

possible interactions between these various roles quickly become bewildering.

Still, it is useful to consider the role the apes play in the personal, economic, and scientific lives of their human sponsors because the way in which those roles have interacted during the last fifteen years sheds light on the meaning of the ape language experiments.

The place to begin is the scientific sphere because it was in this realm that ape and human initially came together. The first thing that strikes one who looks back over the ape language experiments is that it was the graduate students who formed deep bonds with the apes, and not the established scientists. Roger Fouts was a graduate student in Reno, Nevada, when he met Washoe, Penny was a graduate student at Stanford, and Janis Carter was a graduate student at Oklahoma. Premack, Terrace, the Gardners, and Duane Rumbaugh all severed their ties with their pupils when a particular experiment was over. On the other hand, Roger, Penny, and (in a not entirely different way) Janis all at some point had to sever ties with their institutions in order to preserve their relationships with their apes.

The difference between the graduate students' relationships with the apes and the established scientists' relationships with them might in part be accounted for by the fact that the older scientists had scientific identities apart from their work with the apes, while the graduate students did not. Take away the ape work, and the older scientists would still have had some standing in the community, while Penny, Roger, and Janis were solely identified with their apes from the beginnings of their careers. This is not to say that they would not have gone on to do distinguished work had the apes not entered their lives, but rather that the roles the apes played in shaping their lives were all the more important because of their youth and because of the attention their experiments attracted. Further, unlike the older scientists, the graduate students began working with the apes at a time in their lives when people characteristically form deep attachments, and all came to the work with a love of animals. To be sure, a large number of other graduate students worked in the language experiments at different times without having the work take over their lives. But through circumstance and perhaps by design, Roger, Penny, and Janis each ended up as the primary person in an ape's life.

When Roger completed his doctoral work in psychology, he went with Washoe to Oklahoma as part of a package deal. His professional career became entwined with Washoe's destiny. Janis Carter, through circumstance, ended up as Lucy's primary caretaker at a time when Lucy had a celebrated name and Janis was unknown. Indeed, at the time that Janis and Lucy hooked up, Janis was very much at sea about what she wanted to do with her life. Penny was an unknown graduate student when she began teaching Ameslan to Koko, and her growing celebrity sprang from the achievements of her pupil.

The apes may have offered the three young graduate students a cause and a chance for stardom. But through contact with the animals, all three discovered that they had a certain genius for relating to the great apes, something that is just not that easy to do. It would be a mistake to underestimate the satisfaction of discovering that you can relate to and master these strong, independent, and intelligent animals.

And so, if the apes played inordinate roles in the scientific lives of these graduate students, science was still somewhat muddied by circumstances relating to the students' relative youth and inexperience, and also by the attention the apes and the experiments received. Indeed, while Washoe was well known, Roger struggled through several rewrites before the Gardners finally accepted his dissertation. Without yet having been awarded his PhD, Roger came to Oklahoma as a lowly instructor.

Also evident from the beginning was a potential conflict between what might be described as the ideals of many of the researchers and the compromises they had to accept in order to work with apes in captivity.

For instance, the decision to find a chimp to replace Sequoyah must have been difficult for Roger, who believed that chimps should not be separated from their mothers, but who also did not want to see his NSF grant go up in smoke.

On numerous occasions Roger Fouts has asserted that the principal differences between human and chimp derive from the physiological aspects of spoken language. He went on from there to state that chimps would someday find themselves the subject of civil rights battles. Not too many years after making those statements, Roger found himself in the middle of a custody battle with Lemmon concerned with the question of who *owned* Washoe. However, the implications of Roger's earlier statements is that no one has the right to own Washoe.

There is every indication that Roger was sensitive to these contradictions. Indeed, he explored various avenues for getting Washoe back to Africa, where she had been born. Before the question of Washoe's destiny came up, there was the question of the justification for using her in a scientific experiment, and here again I can recall conversations with Roger which suggested that he was very much aware that the substance of the language work with Washoe contradicted the premise that justified using her in an experiment.

In the related field of research on dolphin language use, there are a couple of incidents which show how those feelings surface. Two researchers working with Louis Herman released two dolphins who had been part of Herman's experiment in exploring dolphin language abilities because they felt people had no justification for capturing and using the animals this way. John Lilly attempted to devise an experiment exploring dolphins' higher abilities that was predicated on the dolphin's consent to be part of the experiment (the dolphin initiated all interchanges by pressing an underwater plate with its nose). The fact is that the question of the premises of experimentation is very much on the minds of researchers exploring the abilities of what are perceived to be the smartest animals.

I don't want to overstate the importance of the role this dilemma played in Roger's decisions: given that he and Washoe were in a real world with few alternatives and not in an ethics seminar, I don't imagine that Roger spent too much time thinking up elaborate rationales for his actions. But I can't help wondering whether this tension aroused guilt and acted as a constraint on the way in which Roger pursued his science.

The interplay of emotions and motivations in Roger's relationship with Washoe must be quite complex. Washoe's performance in language spectaculars such as the intergenerational experiments attempted by Roger had the potential to bring fame and fortune to both Roger and Washoe (as well as provide fodder for the argument that Washoe is really one of us); thus, pursuing such an experiment worked to protect Washoe's future, given her compromised circumstance of living in captivity in the United States. On the other hand, Roger was not entirely comfortable with the stress that what he perceived as scientific exactness placed on Washoe. For instance, the rule that no human could sign in the presence of Washoe and her child only served to make Washoe wonder why nobody would talk to her anymore. When I visited Washoe and Loulis with Roger, he took pity on her and furtively signed to her when Loulis was distracted. The results thus were unsatisfactory from all points of view.

Janis Carter was never a figure in ape language experimentation, but it would at first appear that she has gone to the greatest lengths to follow through on the implications of the work. That is to say that, acting on her judgment that there was no justification for keeping Lucy in captivity, she went to extremes to attempt to give Lucy her birthright—life as a wild chimp.

From the beginning, Janis Carter reacted against the ways in which scientific considerations dictated the treatment of captive chimps. She fought with Lemmon about what she perceived to be unnecessarily callous treatment of the chimps. In fact, her reaction against the conditions at the Institute for Primate Studies effectively precluded the possibility of her becoming a scientist by studying captive chimps.

However, Janis frankly admits that she also finds it difficult to let go of the chimps (something that is not helped by continuing uncertainties about their future in The Gambia). While it is true that the chimps need a prime minister to negotiate with the outside world, Janis said during my visit, "At this point I need them more than they need me."

It is easy to understand why Janis would need them, and why she would find it hard to let go, and it is candid of her to admit it. But the dilemma still remains. How do you follow through on your ideals when every temporal and personal consideration pulls you in a contrary direction?

Janis has given eight years of her life to Lucy and the other chimps, and anyone who has had to deal with her can testify to the ferocity of her devotion. But that very ferocity raises questions about whose best interests have been served. A clear-eyed look at the situation in The Gambia tells you that Janis is more than the chimps' elected prime minister; she is their de facto owner, and while that relationship might well be beneficial to the chimps, it is also freighted with the baggage she found abhorrent in Oklahoma.

As Lucy's owner, Janis decided not to speak to Lucy again in sign language, or to allow anyone else to speak to Lucy. While I understand Janis's reasoning that sign language set up a special bond between her and Lucy, I still wonder about that decision. Before Janis came along, Lucy had used sign language for several years to communicate with human beings. It was very much a part of her life. When Janis made her decision about sign language, she did not consider whether it was in the interest of scientific investigation; she did not consult any of the many people who had been in Lucy's life earlier; and she did not leave it up to Lucy. Instead, as Lucy's owner, she decided that it was in Lucy's best interest that signing should abruptly stop. It is the kind of fiat that Janis herself might have found arbitrary and destructive were another person to make it. Indeed, what is most disturbing about Ally's being stripped of his name is that none of his keepers can offer him the reassurance that signing seemed to provide at LEMSIP.

Or take another example: were another Janis Carter to have observed Lucy as the pitiful, hairless wreck she describes Lucy as being during those dark months in Abuko, would this Janis Carter have reacted as harshly as Janis herself did to the circumstances of the chimps at the Institute for Primate Studies? Does it make a difference that Janis's heart was in the right place?

Janis knows the sacrifices she has made for the chimps. She knows how few people would be willing to go to the lengths that she has gone to in order to give Lucy a chance to be free. But like the archetypal Jewish mother, she may not see that those sacrifices do not guarantee that the best interests of Lucy have been served at every point. And those sacrifices may obscure the fact that although Janis has devoted her life to Lucy, she has also used Lucy's life to achieve her own fulfillment.

This same dynamic appears to apply as well to Penny's relationship with Koko. When Penny was a graduate student, Koko was a baby gorilla owned by the San Francisco Zoo. Today Penny is well known and has total control over Koko and Michael. In the interim,

Koko went from being the zoo's property to the Gorilla Foundation's (a nonprofit entity Penny set up to buy Koko). To acquire Koko, Penny mounted a campaign in the press to "Save Koko"—the idea being that Koko would die if separated from Penny and returned to the zoo.

It is entirely possible that Koko would have died (Ally's hysterical paralysis when he was separated from his first human mother shows how traumatic separation from a surrogate mother can be), and despite the somewhat confining circumstances she lives in, I do think Koko is better off with Penny than she would be in a zoo. I tend to think that both animals and human beings do better when their guardians are individuals rather than institutions. Still, in 1977, when she mounted the campaign to "Save Koko," Penny was fighting for herself as much as she was fighting for Koko. Penny can be an all-but-irresistible force when she fixes on something she wants. She is very intelligent and very focused, and when I went over this episode during the research for *The Education of Koko*, I felt some sympathy for the zoo officials, who probably had no inkling of what they were up against.

In all my previous writings about the ape language experiments, I have tended to downplay messy details such as custody battles as irrelevant to the true issues at hand. But just as I was wrong to accept at face value Roger's interpretation of Washoe's treatment of Sequoyah, so was it an error to gloss over the mercurially changing relationships between ape and human being, and between one human being and another in each of these cases. For both Roger and Penny the price of their relationship with a great ape was a certain amount of scientific credibility, and their willingness to pay that price is only understandable in view of the role the ape played in each of their lives.

SOME CRITICS have suggested that the importance of the chimps to the financial and professional lives of the experimenters has caused them to see evidence of language that is not really there. I do not believe that this is the case. Were it merely a question of funding or professional standing, Roger and Penny would have pitched their apes overboard long ago, as did Herb Terrace. Both of them are more aware than anyone else that their approach to both collecting and interpreting sign-language data puts them in conflict with, rather than in accord with, the professional juries that make funding decisions. Funding institutions do not tend to reward people who make extravagant claims and extravagant promises. This is not just the case today, it has been the case throughout the history of these experiments. If they were simply in it for the money and the glory, both Roger and Penny would more likely keep devising new experiments with new apes (as other comparative psychologists have done) rather than sticking loyally with their original experimental subjects.

I feel instead that what one analyst called "overgenerous" interpretations flow from the volatile chemistry that occurs when you add young scientists and the ambiguity of language to experiments depending on strong relationships between human beings and animals. In the case of Roger and Penny, the certainty that comes from their intimate knowledge of their ape subjects has acted to erode their patience with the plodding, beetle-browed empiricism of the behavioral sciences.

The problem perhaps is that when ambiguous scientific issues are explored through a relationship, the relationship may ultimately prove more important to the scientists than the conventions of scientific method. For Janis Carter, that relationship proved not only more important than scientific method but also more important than science itself.

At the heart of the matter is the ambiguity of the subject—language—that is being explored. The more established scientists shied away from the ambiguity, abandoning language work and retreating toward what they regarded as more knowable terrain. And they left the apes involved behind in the process. The younger scientists retreated from the ambiguities toward the certainties of their relationships with the apes, compounding the scientific ambiguities in the process.

CHAPTER EIGHTEEN

Poor Relations

IN THE introduction, I suggested that just as an intelligence agent might study railroad movements in East Germany as a clue to Warsaw Pact intentions, another type of intelligence agent might draw some inferences from the flurry of chimp movements during the late seventies and early eighties. What might such inferences be? At first blush, the forces that sent Lucy to Africa were different from those that sent Ally and Nim to LEMSIP. In fact, different forces determined Ally and Nim's trip to LEMSIP from those which governed Ally's return trip to Oklahoma and Nim's trip to Black Beauty Ranch. And different forces still governed Washoe's trip to Ellensburg, and Koko's short trips from the San Francisco Zoo to Stanford to Woodside.

A superficial analysis of these movements would suggest that idealism sent Lucy to Africa while economic necessity sent Ally and Nim to the medical lab. On the other hand, their "rescue" from the medical lab might be seen as the result of an outpouring of humane, animal-loving sentiment. The same quick glance would lead one to the conclusion that Washoe went to Ellensburg because it promised both Roger and Washoe a haven safe from the influence of William Lemmon, and that Koko's various moves were the product of Penny's attempts to find a similar refuge for Koko.

Thus we would have chimps moving because of idealism, economic necessity, humane sentiment, and personal devotion.

Or one could claim that the various chimp movements were determined by whether the animals were viewed as a commodity or as personalities. There is the actual marketplace in which chimps are traded as a commodity. This market gives a value to the chimps that is a product of all the factors that determine the value of the animals —age, sex, breeding potential, experimental history, and so forth. However, sporadically acting on this marketplace and totally skewing an otherwise orderly market are some elusive factors. For instance, for a brief moment, Ally and Nim were transformed from commodities into personalities, and in consequence the economic considerations that had previously governed their movements became irrelevant—in fact they became horrifying.

However, the cynic looking at these chimp movements would note that whether the ape was treated as a commodity or a personality, its movements were still governed by the special interests of the human beings in its life, and that even those people who were treating the apes as personalities still treated them as commodities when the question of ownership arose. I don't think this cynical analysis wholly explains all these chimp movements; it doesn't explain, for example, the campaign to rescue Ally and Nim from the medical lab. This was not a case in which an individual wanted to keep either chimp for his own purposes. In fact, because they were institutionally owned, Ally's and Nim's movements were more affected by large forces in society rather than by more individual self-interest.

Their movement to the medical laboratory reflected the traditional approach humanity takes to the animal world—namely that apes and any other animals are re-sources at our disposal, to be used to solve our prob-lems. It is fair to say that this movement was determined by economic necessity. An interesting and sad observa-tion that can be made about the sale of Ally and Nim to LEMSIP is that the marketplace accorded the two chimps no premium in value despite the intensive and expensive training they had earlier received in sign lan-guage. There were people who wanted to continue to work with Ally and Nim, but no individual or institution would pay a premium sufficient to make it worthwhile for Lemmon to consider the offer. Society, as reflected in the marketplace, said that training chimps to use a human language had no value.

However, the market for apes, as noted above, is not totally efficient. One phone call by a distressed graduate student set into motion a chain of events that put a pre-mium on Ally and Nim (but not on Booee or Bruno or any of the other less articulate, less well-known members of their group), and that made it far too expen-sive for LEMSIP to keep the chimps. Ally and Nim went to LEMSIP because their anatomical similarities to hu-mankind made them useful for batch testing; they left LEMSIP once the world was reminded of their behav-ioral similarities to people.

The furor over the question of Ally and Nim's fate showed that there are significant numbers of people who are uncomfortable with a commodity approach to our fellow creatures. A lot of different types of people—an-tivivisectionists, animal rights advocates, and cat lovers, to name but a few—became exercised about the fact that Ally and Nim were to be assaulted with hepatitis B virus. The fact that the two chimps had been taught sign lan-guage offered each of these groups an opportunity they could not ignore, but dogs, cats, or horses would have elicited equal if not greater responses from the public had their stories been personalized the way Ally and Nim's was. The outcry over Ally and Nim was not an endorsement of the fact that they might know language (although this circumstance framed the issue for the general public) so much as it was a lament over our treatment of animals in general.

The problem is that while there are many dedicated animal lovers (I include myself among them), the role of their sentiment in society seems to be to expiate society's accumulating guilt about the way we treat the world that formed us and houses us. The trouble with such a phenomenon is that, as is the case with any token redemptive act, its function is to maintain the status quo. Which brings us back to Mahoney's remark: "People make a phone call and think that they have done something for the chimps." The phone call makes you feel good, but it does not change an attitude toward nature which is profoundly embedded in our society, and which will continue to determine the lives of other chimps and other animals, even if Ally and Nim have been "rescued."

A cause célèbre transformed Ally and Nim from commodities into symbols through which society might redeem its abuse of the natural world. But from Nim's point of view, being a symbol is not all that wonderful a job. In essence he is now hostage to our collective conscience—too celebrated to be obviously abused, but not powerful enough to command the resources that would give him the life he needs. Nim's material future is secure—the Fund for Animals has enough money to pay his keep in perpetuity—but he lives in a type of suspense. That he is at Black Beauty Ranch is a function not so much of his needs as of our needs. Ally, who lost his name in the confusion that followed his role as a symbol, faces a more uncertain future.

And so it was not individual self-interest but collective self-interest that governed Ally's and Nim's movements about the country. The need to exploit them for their anatomical similarities to humanity led them to LEMSIP, and our collective need to assuage our guilt about this approach to the animal world led them out of LEMSIP.

This is why I think their saga is like a chimpanzee pilgrim's progress in which they must traverse an ambiguous moral terrain. Ally and Nim have been propelled about the countryside by incarnations of the various conflicting approaches we appear to take toward the animal world.

But these approaches are not, in truth, conflicting—they are complementary. "Saving" Ally and Nim does not affect the business as usual that has put the 1,700 other captive chimps in the United States at risk. Quite the contrary: saving Ally and Nim is necessary to the psychic balance of the system that puts those chimps at risk. Saving Ally and Nim allows us to ignore Booee and Bruno and the poor chimps being shot up with AIDS virus or otherwise used in terminal experiments.

Animal rights and animal welfare advocates argue that using chimps or other animals as surrogates in research and testing is as evil as Nazi medical experiments on concentration camp victims. Proponents of using animals for research argue that antivivisectionist sentiment is profoundly misanthropic and antiscientific. Both sides can make a case: one shudders to think what kind of a society we would be if people did not react with horror when confronted with the terror and mutilation inflicted on animals in the name of experimentation and testing. On the other hand, how many of our vaccines, FDA test procedures, and other health precautions are we really willing to give up as the price of animal rights? As a society, are we really willing to increase uncertainty and increase risk for the sake of other species? As a society, are we even willing to decrease our standard of living for the sake of starving people in the Third World? For the sake of hungry Americans? For the sake of the homeless person on the park bench or in front of your house? How many ordinary Americans would rather be unemployed than work in a factory that produces nuclear weapons?

How many people in blighted areas will even vote against the interests of an employer who poisons their own air or water?

It is questions like these that gave rise to our typical response: a symbolic gesture of one sort or another, something that will not disrupt the momentum of our lives. But in truth we would rather not have to face what goes on in the laboratory that produces cosmetics, or in the refugee camps of Ethiopia.

People tend to live for the short term, even if the short term throws a cloud over their long-term prospects. In the case of apes, a constellation of short-term considerations of health and scientific convenience create pressures to treat apes like a commodity rather than a creatures with rights. It may be that we can't afford to treat them any other way. What this means for chimps should by now be clear. When I began working on *Apes, Men, and Language*, I suspected that this was the case. Now I am certain of it.

THE TRAGEDY of chimpanzees is that while they are close enough to being human to attract our attention, they present us with a mirror that we find unwelcome. They have a smaller brain, they are excitable, their behavior seems to mock our veneer of civilization. They compound the tragedy by growing up into chimpanzees, and not into complaisant pets, or eager would-be human beings.

When I first heard about attempts to teach sign language to chimpanzees, my reaction was that if these attempts were successful, they would alter our conventional definitions of human nature. That is why I wanted to write *Apes, Men, and Language*. At that point, I was not that interested in apes. In fact, when I first began research, I believed that a more likely candidate for learning language would be the dolphin. My opinion on this matter changed once I became acquainted with the practical difficulties and expense of working with an animal that lives underwater. (In fact in Hawaii, Louis Herman is pursuing a very interesting ongoing experiment with dolphins, but the practical difficulties of working underwater have not yet been conquered to the degree that would permit the wide-ranging, spontaneous conversations that sign language permits with apes.) However, I suspect that both in the popular mind and in science, news of dolphin breakthroughs in language would be better received than has been news of attempts to teach apes language.

Dolphins are beautiful, with skull characteristics—a broad, high forehead—that we associate with nobility and intelligence. Their brains are larger than ours and endowed with characteristics we associate with intelligence. Moreover, most people associate dolphins with stories about their helping lost seamen or saving drowning children. You don't hear stories about dolphins attacking people or biting fingers. Dolphins are the kind of creature we would rather be associated with should we decide to broaden the membership in our exclusive club (another question altogether). Chimps are just not our kind of people. They remind us of an evolutionary history that it seems we would like to forget, and they are a former competitor for food and territory to boot.

The pro-whale predisposition is apparent in the myriad groups engaged in the entirely worthy cause of saving the whales and dolphins. Greenpeace and other save-the-whale groups get support from a broad spectrum of people. Virtually the only opposition comes, as might be expected, from the whaling industry, and from fishermen who find dolphins a nuisance.

Although some of the great apes are as imperiled as any species of whale, our poor relations inspire no such broad-based support devoted exclusively to saving them. Shirley McGreel's organization, the International Primate Protection League, does what it can on a shoestring budget, and the big conservation groups certainly try to help, but despite publicity about their plight, the apes do not inspire the same emotional response as the whales—that is, until you get to know them.

But there is some question about how well we want to get to know the apes, except in terms of useful anatomical similarities. For instance, there is still a great deal of question about which of the great apes is our closest relative, as well as in what ways genetic differences between people and different apes make apes either useful or not useful as human surrogates in research. None of this ambiguity has halted either research or testing that involves using chimps as surrogates for humans. If anything, it has spurred the search to find the answers to these biological questions.

There is a similar ambiguity with respect to the behavioral communalities between man and ape. For instance, sign language unlocked a means of communicating across the species gap that spoken language would not permit. Some scientists took a look at this and wondered whether the same approach might work with autistic children. They did not worry about whether the chimps' communications satisfied every last definition of language. Rather they saw that sign language might offer a way around a physiological or neurological roadblock in humans just as it did in chimps. And it worked. In this case, chimps turned out to be a useful behavioral surrogate for people.

We are not above acknowledging our genetic relationship with apes short of absolute certainty if acknowledging that relationship helps us to deal with human problems, and we are not above occasional de facto acknowledgments of behavioral similarities either, but on the question of language, it seems that all of a sudden we want all or nothing, and that we reserve the right to decide what *all* means depending on what apes fail to do.

* * *

IT IS entirely possible that the hostile climate of the past few years is as much a product of the times as were the heady early days of ape language studies. Ultimately the behavioral sciences may digest the critics and look at the work with some perspective. There are glimmerings that this is beginning to happen. Ristau and Robbins's appraisal of language in the great apes and Alison Jolley's new edition of *The Evolution of Primate Behavior* both look at Terrace's work with Nim as one idiosyncratic experiment rather than as the final word on ape language capacity.

There are also glimmerings that scientists may take a second look at their original work with apes. In 1984 Duane Rumbaugh reported that Lana behaves differently from the other chimps in the main chimp colony at Emory-Yerkes, where she has been since Rumbaugh finished his work with her. He has noted that she is more studied in the way she reacts and goes about things. If the language she learned were nothing more than a means to get a reward, then it would follow that Yerkish should not have had any general effect on the way she relates to the world. Rumbaugh seems to think that perhaps being taught Yerkish did have some effect on the way Lana processes information and relates to her environment.

While only Lyn Miles and the Rumbaughs have government funding for language work with apes at the moment, there is a veritable renaissance in the study of the cognitive behavior of all types of animals. Indeed, many of the psychologists who abandoned the study of language with apes have moved into the study of ape cognition, ostensibly because aspects of cognition more easily lend themselves to empirical study.

While I wish these scientists good luck, I can't help but wonder whether experiments in the higher cognitive behavior of apes and other animals will ultimately founder on the same shoals of subjectivity and irresoluteness that beached the language experiments. There is currently no greater consensus about the definition of intelligence than there is about the definition of language. Moreover, so long as the questions about language remain unsettled, cognitive scientists are going to be forever at sea about what their discoveries mean. As the Dahlem Conference (cited in Chapter Five) showed, cognitive scientists looked to the language experiments for corroborative evidence, and what they found was Herb Terrace saying, don't look here for any evidence that apes are capable of expressing abstract thoughts through language. Finally the study of cognitive behavior is not immune from the philosophical-religious forces that intruded on the study of language.

We have a great deal invested in the belief that language and rationality endow us with the prerogative to use the planet and everything on it as we see fit. On the other hand, science continually produces people who look around at other creatures and ask, why isn't there continuity between animal and human behavior just as there is between animal and human anatomy? Thus the logical implications of evolution continually butt up against the way we need to see the world. So far the loser in this ongoing conflict has been science, and the victims of this particular chapter of the conflict have been a few captive chimpanzees.

In the long run, we are the victims of a skewed view of our relationship with the rest of the natural order. We treat everything besides ourselves as a commodity whose value is determined by the short-term considerations of the marketplace, but how do we know that the market is efficient enough to assign a true value to everything in nature? Are we endangering or eliminating organisms that may be vital to our own long-term survival? It is hubris to assume that science can answer this question. This is why I think that the way we view and treat our poor relations has considerable meaning for us. Not because humanity will die out if the other great apes die out (though a world so overpopulated that it had no forest refuges for the great apes might be a world in deep peril), but because the exaggerated response these animals elicit from people reveals the way we look at nature and at ourselves.

And what the wanderings of the sign-language-using apes show us is the dark side of humanism. Humanism, the notion that man is the noblest product of creation, responsible for the correct stewardship of the planet, carries with it a necessary blindness to the nature of evolution. The immediate price of this pride is a sense of our identity. In the long run it could be our survival.

INDEX

EUGENE LINDEN has been an active observer of the ape language experiments for fifteen years. His book *Apes, Men, and Language* has become a classic in the field and is now printed in eight languages. *Newsweek* wrote of it: "What Linden says about chimps and language is fascinating. He manages adroitly a short course in linguistics—a complicated subject." Linden is also the author of three other books as well as many articles. A graduate of Yale University, he now lives in New York City with his wife and daughter.